CHARACTER SONGS
FROM
MUSICAL THEATRE

MEN'S EDITION

30 SONGS
FROM FEATURED CHARACTER ROLES

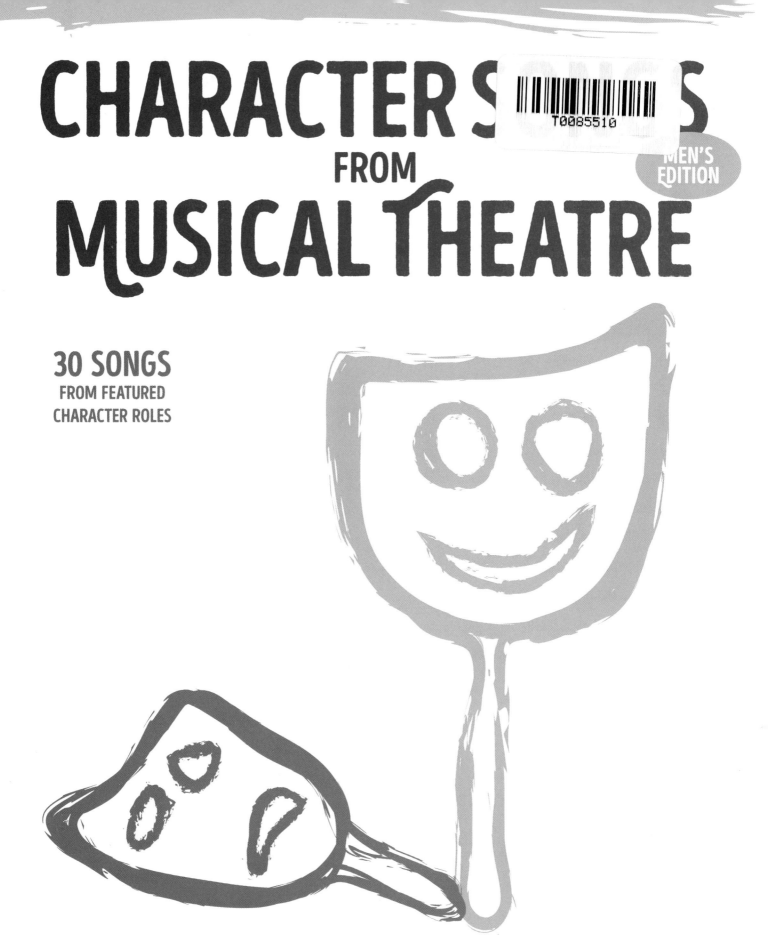

ISBN 978-1-4950-9952-6

HAL•LEONARD®
7777 W. BLUEMOUND RD. P.O. BOX 13819 MILWAUKEE, WI 53213

Visit Hal Leonard Online at
www.halleonard.com

CONTENTS BY SONG

4	The Ballad of Billy M'Caw	*Cats*
10	The Ballad of Farquaad	*Shrek The Musical*
22	Boy for Sale	*Oliver!*
24	Bring Me My Bride	*A Funny Thing Happened on the Way to the Forum*
38	Brush Up Your Shakespeare	*Kiss Me, Kate*
44	Friend Like Me	*Aladdin*
54	Gaston	*Beauty and the Beast: The Broadway Musical*
31	Grand Knowing You	*She Loves Me*
62	Haben sie Gehört Das Deutsche Band?	*The Producers*
66	Heil Myself	*The Producers*
72	I Am Aldolpho	*The Drowsy Chaperone*
76	I'm Calm	*A Funny Thing Happened on the Way to the Forum*
80	I'm Not Wearing Underwear Today	*Avenue Q*
82	If I Were King of the Forest	*The Wizard of Oz*
91	If You Were Gay	*Avenue Q*
84	In Old Bavaria	*The Producers*
86	It Ain't Necessarily So	*Porgy and Bess*
96	Ladies in Their Sensitivities	*Sweeney Todd*
100	Les Poissons	*The Little Mermaid – A Broadway Musical*
105	Me	*Beauty and the Beast: The Broadway Musical*
110	Mister Cellophane	*Chicago*
118	My Unfortunate Erection	*The 25th Annual Putnam County Spelling Bee*
115	On This Night of a Thousand Stars	*Evita*
126	Quasimodo	*When Pigs Fly*
130	Reviewing the Situation	*Oliver!*
141	A Secretary Is Not a Toy	*How to Succeed in Business Without Really Trying*
148	Sit Down You're Rockin' the Boat	*Guys and Dolls*
154	Springtime for Hitler	*The Producers*
159	Where Was I When They Passed Out the Luck?	*Minnie's Boys*
166	You Won't Succeed on Broadway	*Monty Python's Spamalot*

CONTENTS BY SHOW

THE 25TH ANNUAL PUTNAM COUNTY SPELLING BEE
118   My Unfortunate Erection

ALADDIN
44   Friend Like Me

AVENUE Q
80   I'm Not Wearing Underwear Today
91   If You Were Gay

BEAUTY AND THE BEAST: THE BROADWAY MUSICAL
54   Gaston
105   Me

CATS
4   The Ballad of Billy M'Caw

CHICAGO
110   Mister Cellophane

THE DROWSY CHAPERONE
72   I Am Aldolpho

EVITA
115   On This Night of a Thousand Stars

A FUNNY THING HAPPENED ON THE WAY TO THE FORUM
24   Bring Me My Bride
76   I'm Calm

GUYS AND DOLLS
148   Sit Down You're Rockin' the Boat

HOW TO SUCCEED IN BUSINESS WITHOUT REALLY TRYING
141   A Secretary Is Not a Toy

KISS ME, KATE
38   Brush Up Your Shakespeare

THE LITTLE MERMAID – A BROADWAY MUSICAL
100   Les Poissons

MINNIE'S BOYS
159   Where Was I When They Passed Out the Luck?

MONTY PYTHON'S SPAMALOT
166   You Won't Succeed on Broadway

OLIVER!
22   Boy for Sale
130   Reviewing the Situation

PORGY AND BESS
86   It Ain't Necessarily So

THE PRODUCERS
62   Haben sie Gehört Das Deutsche Band?
66   Heil Myself
84   In Old Bavaria
154   Springtime for Hitler

SHE LOVES ME
31   Grand Knowing You

SHREK THE MUSICAL
10   The Ballad of Farquaad

SWEENEY TODD
96   Ladies in Their Sensitivities

WHEN PIGS FLY
126   Quasimodo

THE WIZARD OF OZ
82   If I Were King of the Forest

THE BALLAD OF BILLY M'CAW
from *Cats*

Music by Andrew Lloyd Webber
Text by T.S. Eliot

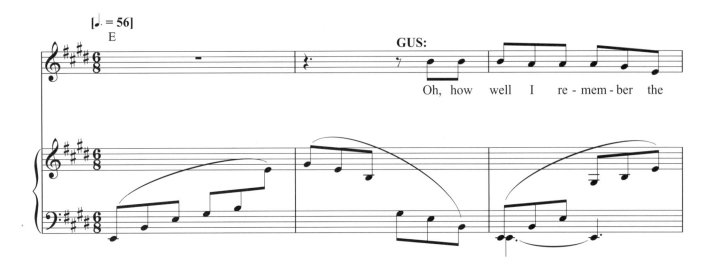

Oh, how well I re-mem-ber the

old Bull and Bush, Where we used to go down on a Sat-ta-day night, Where, when

an-y-thing hap-pened, it come with a rush, For the boss, Mis-ter Clark, he was

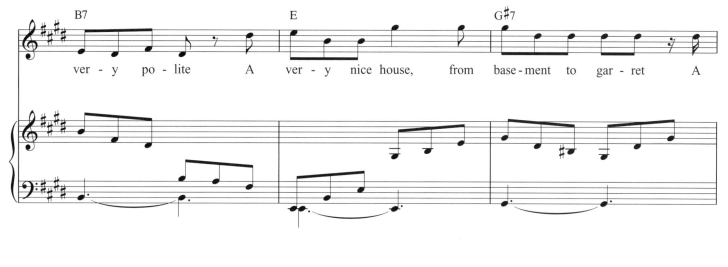

very polite A very nice house, from base-ment to gar-ret A

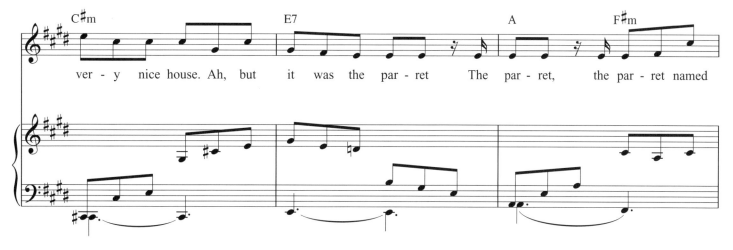

very nice house. Ah, but it was the par-ret The par-ret, the par-ret named

Bil-ly M'-Caw that brought all those folk to the bar. Ah, he was the life of the bar. Of a

Colla voce

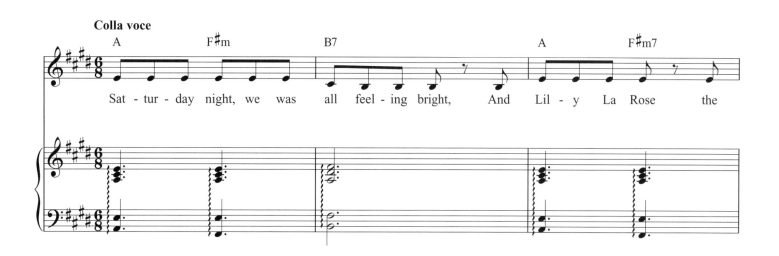

Sat-tur-day night, we was all feel-ing bright, And Lil-y La Rose the

A Tempo

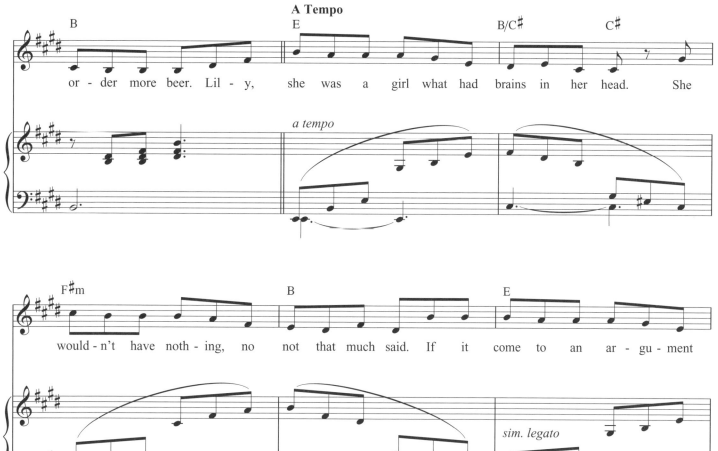

or - der more beer. Lil - y, she was a girl what had brains in her head. She

would - n't have noth - ing, no not that much said. If it come to an ar - gu - ment

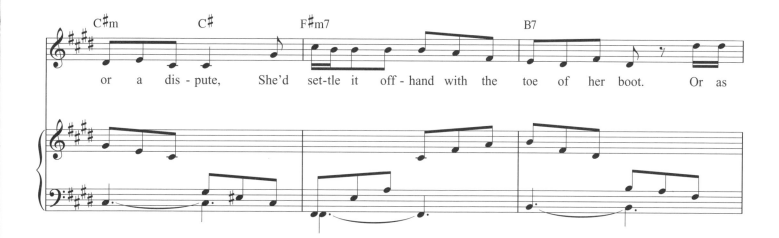

or a dis - pute, She'd set-tle it off - hand with the toe of her boot. Or as

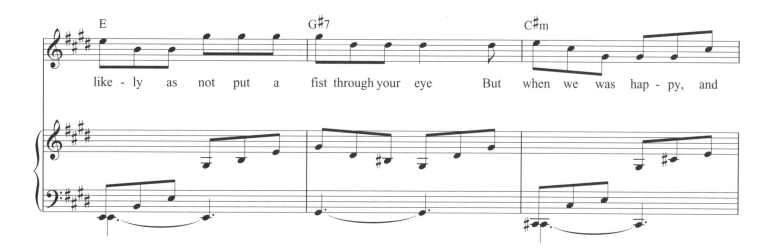

like - ly as not put a fist through your eye But when we was hap - py, and

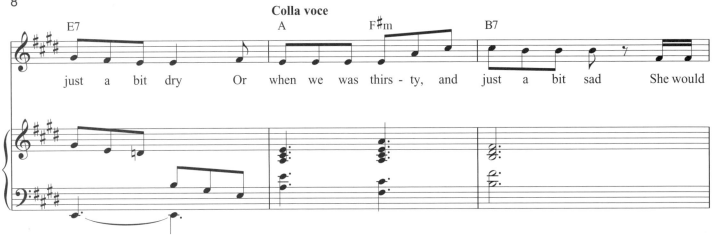

Colla voce

just a bit dry Or when we was thirs - ty, and just a bit sad She would

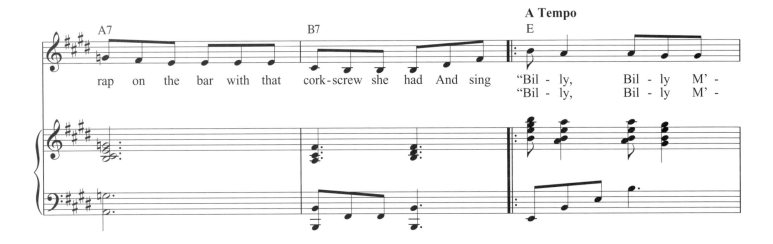

A Tempo

rap on the bar with that cork-screw she had And sing "Bil - ly, Bil - ly M' -
"Bil - ly, Bil - ly M' -

Caw! _____ Come give us a tune on your pas - to - ral flute!" And
Caw! _____ Come give us a tune on your mo - ley gui - tar!" And

Bil - ly'd strike up on his pas - to - ral flute. And Bil - ly'd strike up on his
Bil - ly'd strike up on his mo - ley gui - tar. And Bil - ly'd strike up on his

Colla voce

pas - tor - al flute.)
mo - ley gui - tar)
And then we'd feel balm - y, in each eye a tear And e -

mo - tion would make us all or - der more beer. or - der more beer.

A Tempo

Bil - ly! Bil - ly M' - Caw!_____ Come give us a tune on your mo - ley gui - tar! Ah!

He was the life of the bar._____ Yes He was the life of the bar.

THE BALLAD OF FARQUAAD

from *Shrek The Musical*

Words by David Lindsay-Abaire
Music by Jeanine Tesori

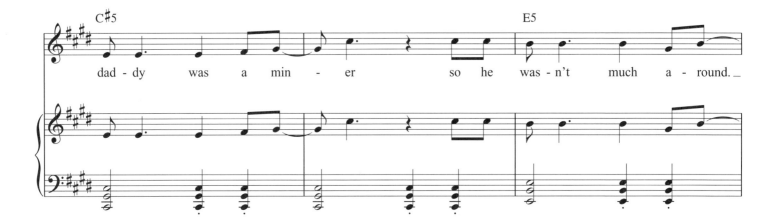

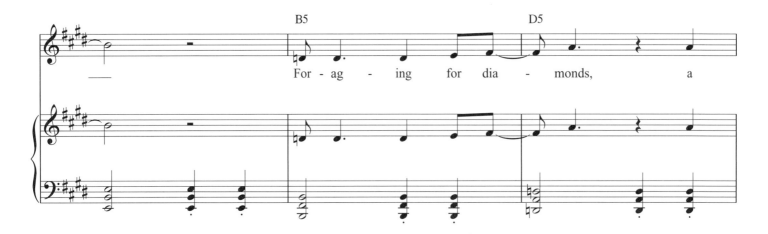

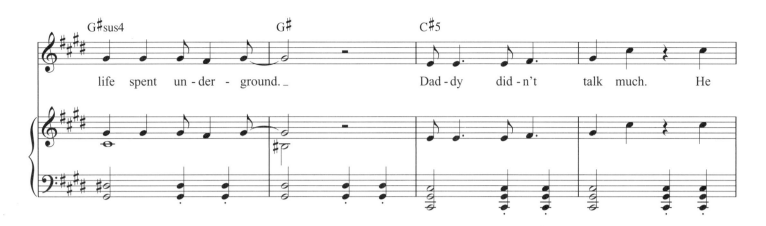

life spent un-der-ground. Dad-dy did-n't talk much. He

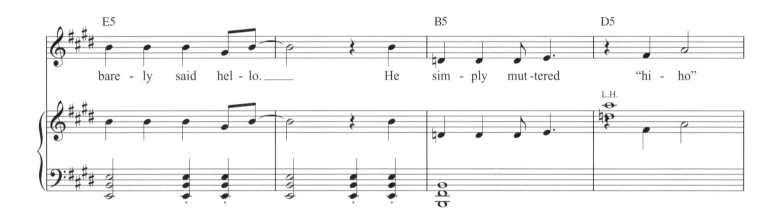

bare-ly said hel-lo. He sim-ply mut-tered "hi-ho"

and off to work he'd go. Dad-dy was

grump-y. My ma-ma was a prin-cess who

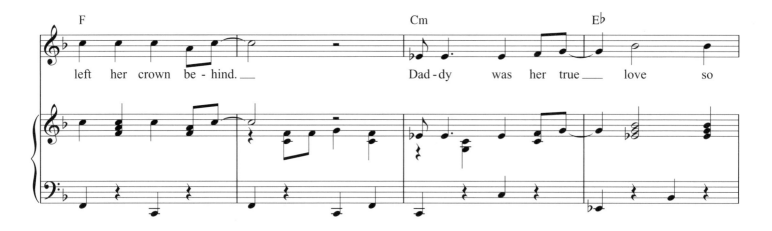

left her crown be-hind. ___ Dad-dy was her true ___ love so

Ma-ma did-n't mind. ___ I nev-er knew my ma-ma, but she

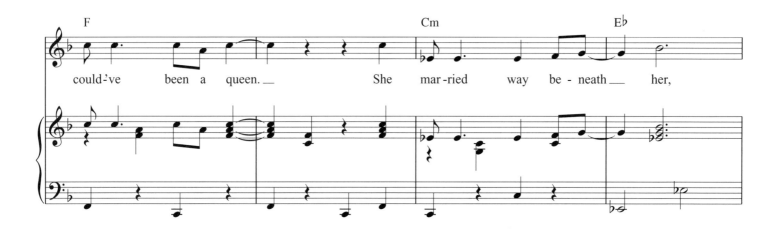

could've been a queen. ___ She mar-ried way be-neath ___ her,

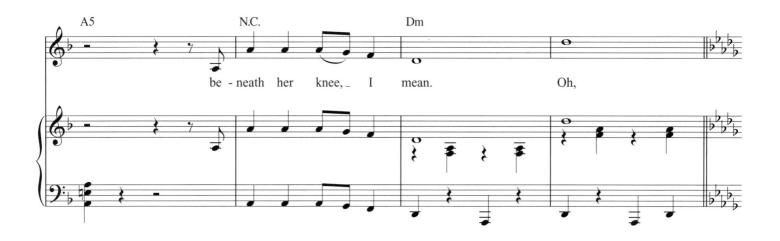

be-neath her knee, I mean. Oh,

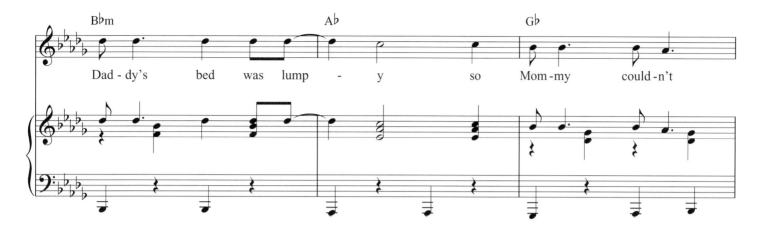

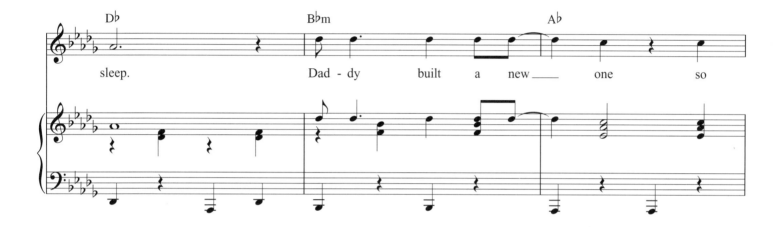

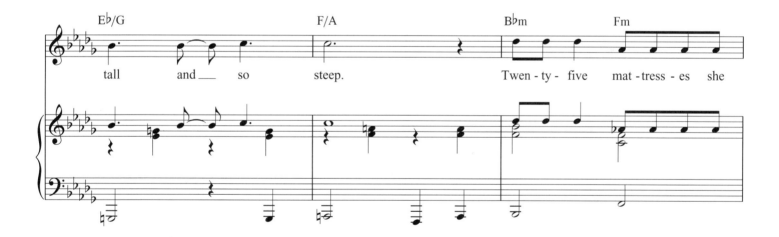

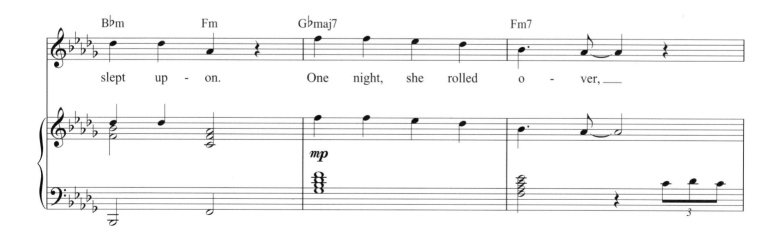

and Ma - ma was gone.

So Dad - dy was grump - y.

Me and my old man, a tale as old as

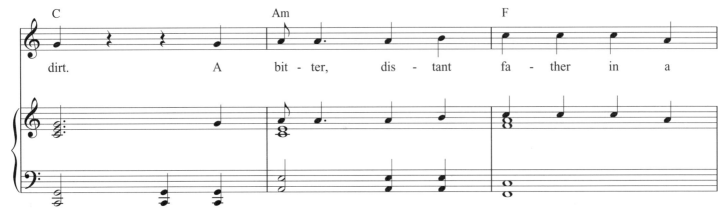

dirt. A bit - ter, dis - tant fa - ther in a

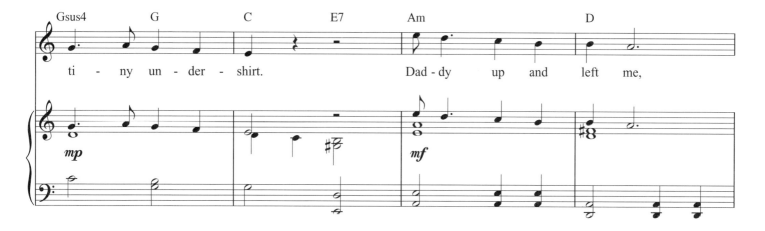

ti - ny un - der - shirt. Dad - dy up and left me,

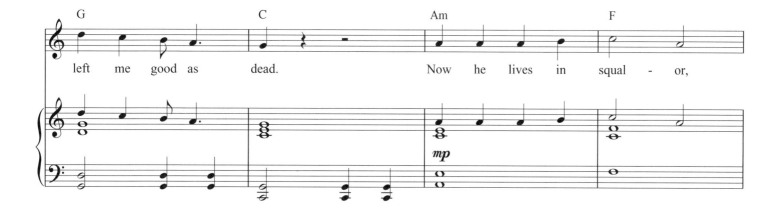

left me good as dead. Now he lives in squal - or,

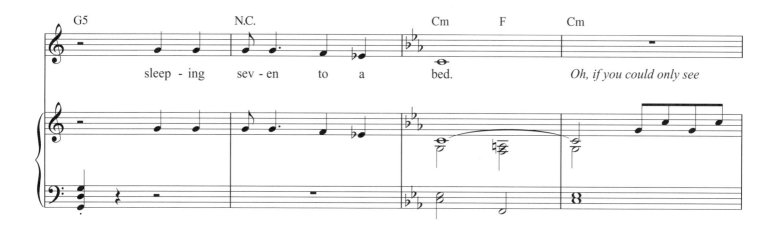

sleep - ing sev - en to a bed. *Oh, if you could only see*

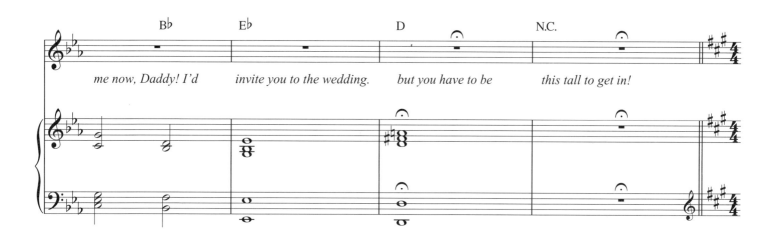

me now, Daddy! I'd *invite you to the wedding.* *but you have to be* *this tall to get in!*

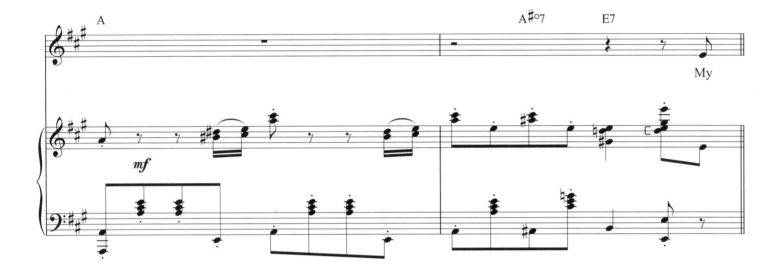

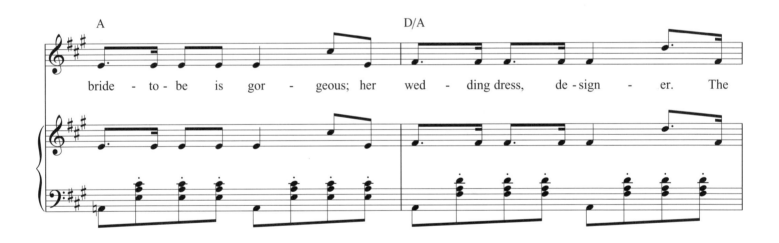

bride - to - be is gor - geous; her wed - ding dress, de - sign - er. The

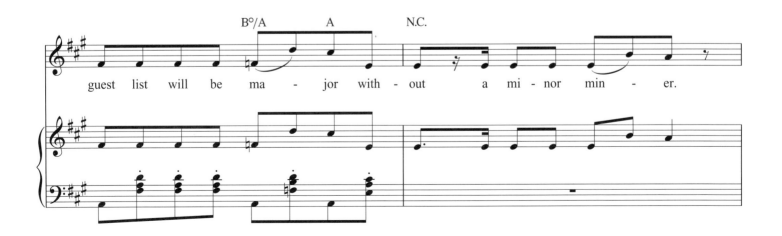

guest list will be ma - jor with - out a mi - nor min - er.

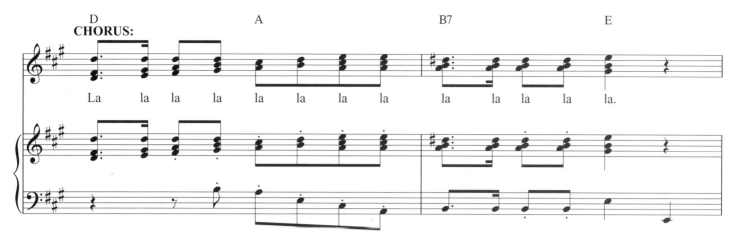

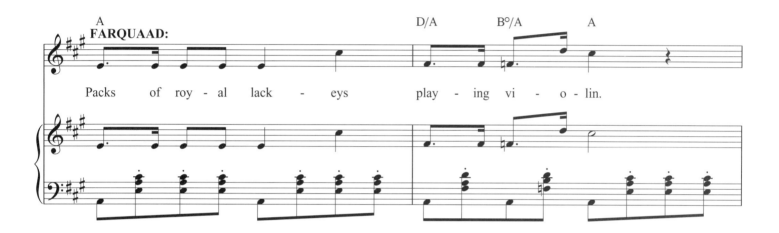

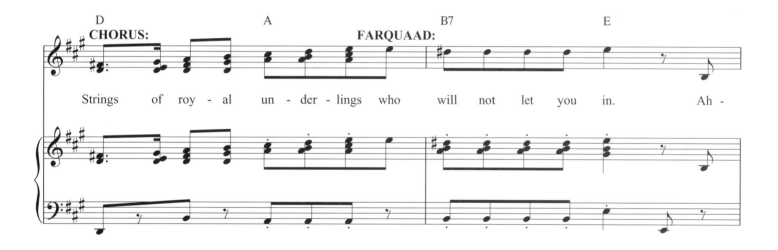

18

car - riage, twen - ty stal - lions with a
CHORUS: Tricked - out car - riage, twen - ty stal - lions

coach - man named Ra - oul. Big re -
with a coach - man named Ra - oul.

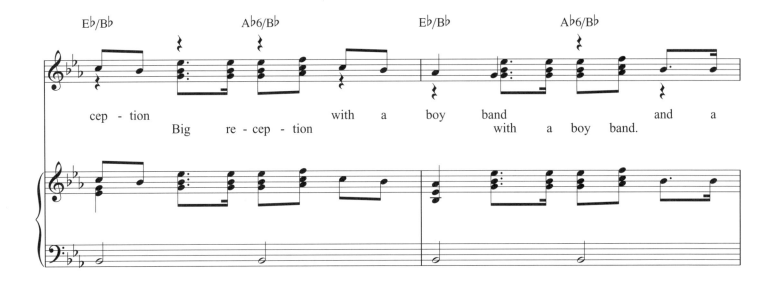

cep - tion with a boy band and a
Big re - cep - tion with a boy band.

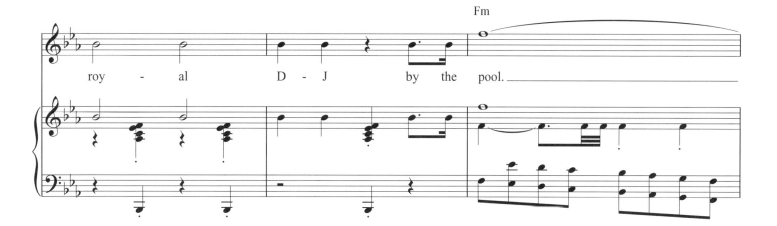

roy - al D - J by the pool.

Yes!

Tempo I (♩ = 80)

I can see my fu - ture, and so it shall be done.

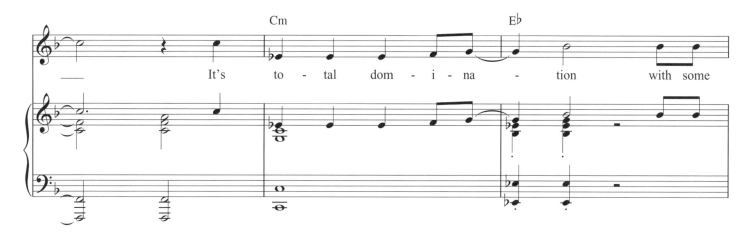

It's to - tal dom - i - na - tion with some

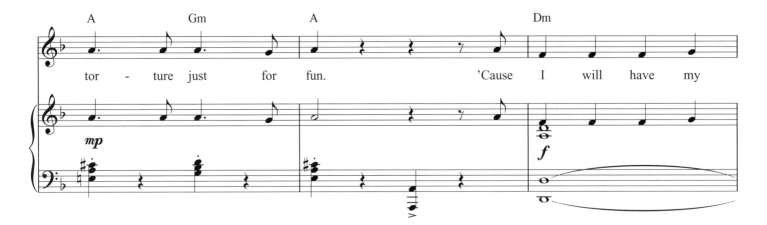

tor - ture just for fun. 'Cause I will have my

wed - ding, and I will __ have a queen. __

Once I get that crown on you will get the guil - lo - tine. __

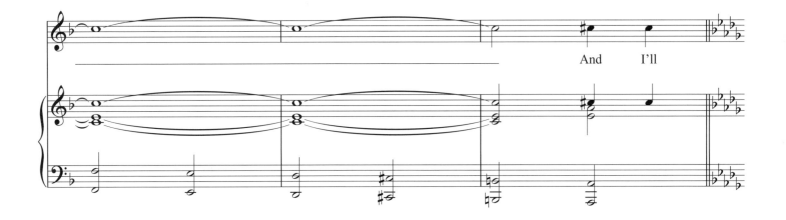

And I'll

pun - ish you, Dad - dy, 'cause I'm all grown up and big - ger than you'll ev - er

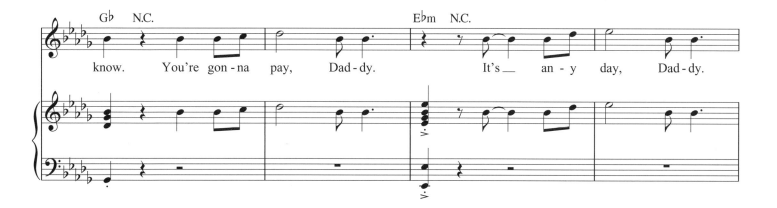

know. You're gon - na pay, Dad - dy. It's __ an - y day, Dad - dy.

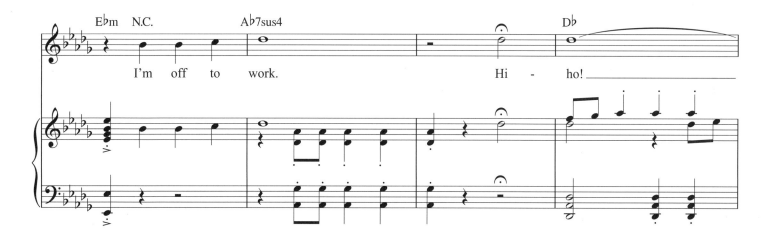

I'm off to work. Hi - ho! _____

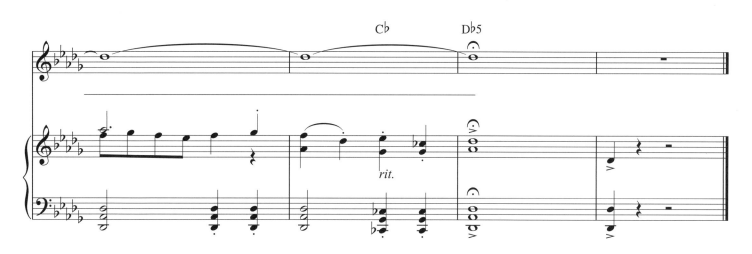

BOY FOR SALE
from the Columbia Pictures - Romulus film *Oliver!*

Words and Music by
Lionel Bart

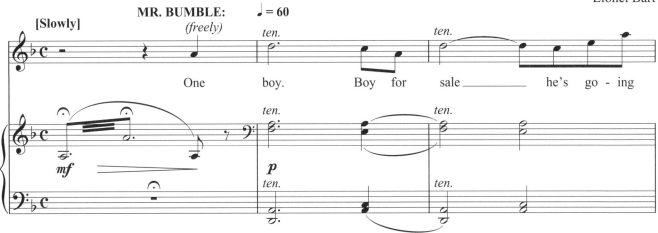

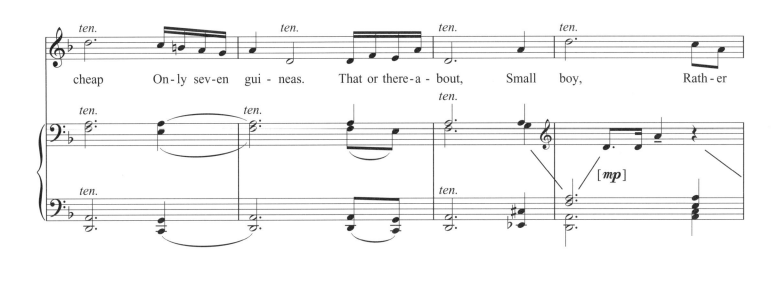

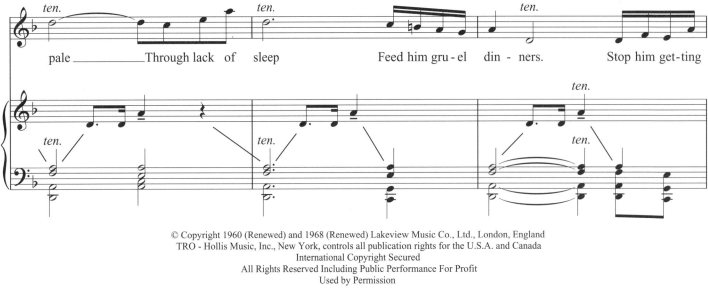

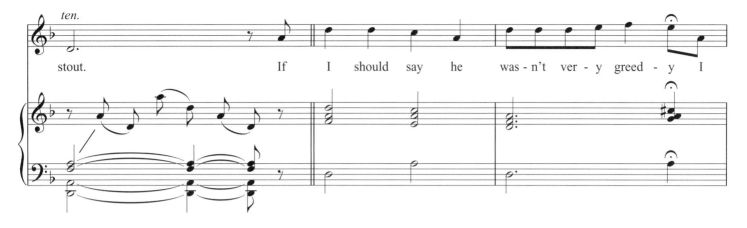

stout. If I should say he was-n't ver - y greed - y I

could not, I'd be tell - ing you a tale. One boy Boy for

sale Come take a peep Have you ev - er seen as Nice a boy for

(Spoken:) Liberal terms, Mister Sowerberry, – Liberal terms.

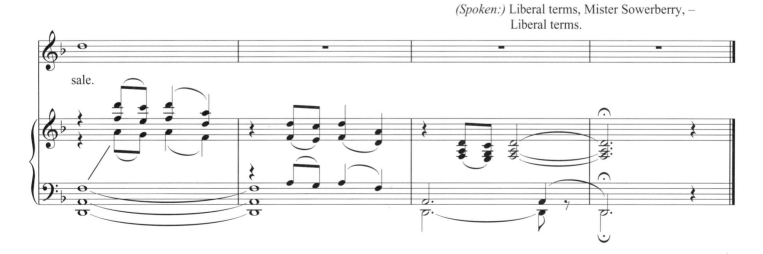

sale.

BRING ME MY BRIDE
from *A Funny Thing Happened on the Way to the Forum*

Words and Music by
Stephen Sondheim

can - not be de - layed! There are lands to con - quer, Cit - ies to loot And

peo - ple to de - grade! Look at these arms! Look at this chest!

Look at them! Not to men - tion the rest! E - ven I am im -

pressed! My bride! My bride! Come bring to me my bride! My

* Ensemble lyrics have been slightly adapted for this solo edition.

lust for her no long-er can be de - nied! Con - vey the news! I

have no time to lose! There are towns to plun - der, Tem-ples to burn And

wom - en to a - buse! Look at that foot! Look at that heel!

Mark the mag - ni - fi - cent mus - cles of steel! I am my i -

deal!   I,   Mi - les Glo - ri -

o - sus, _____   I,   slaugh-ter - er   of thou - sands,

I,   op - pres-sor of   the meek,   Sub-du - er of   the weak,   De-grad - er of the

Greek,   De - stroy - er of   the Turk,   Must hur - ry   back   to

work! I, Mi - les Glo - ri - o - sus,

I, par - a - gon of vir - tues, I, in war the most ad-

mired, In wit the most in - spired, In love the most de-

sired, In dress the best dis - played, I am a pa - rade!

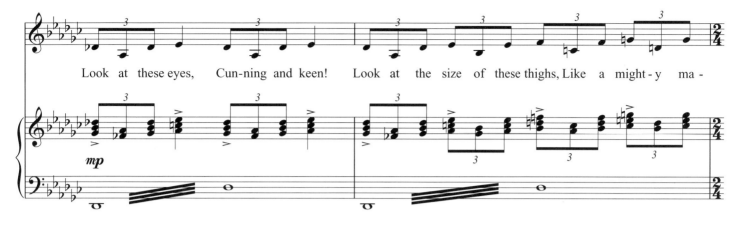

Look at these eyes, Cun-ning and keen! Look at the size of these thighs, Like a might-y ma-

chine! My bride! My bride! In -

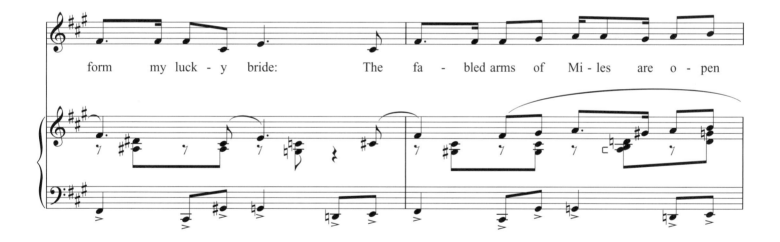

form my luck-y bride: The fa - bled arms of Mi - les are o - pen

wide! Make haste! Make haste! I

have no time to waste! There are shrines I should be sack-ing,

Ribs I should be crack-ing, Eyes to gouge and boo-ty to di-vide!

Bring me my bride! _____ Bring me my

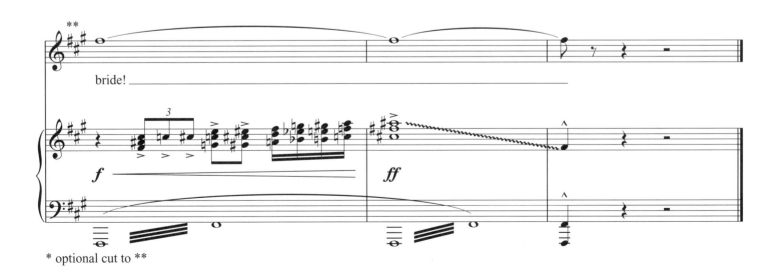

bride! _____

* optional cut to **

GRAND KNOWING YOU
from *She Loves Me*

Words by Sheldon Harnick
Music by Jerry Bock

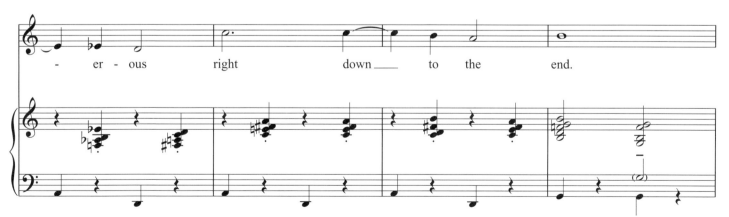

Please don't grieve watch - ing me leave. That ___

___ would be much too pain - ful to stand.

It's been fun now ___ I must run. But ___

___ it's been grand per - fect - ly grand.

Rubato - Slowly

Il - o - na____ fare - well, cher - ie. Be

brave. Chin up. It's been sub - lime. You must - n't____ waste a pre-cious

mo - ment o - ver me. You don't have time.____

(falsetto)

Just re - mem - ber when you're lone - ly or____ blue____

(falsetto)

there's a hol-low in my pil-low for _____

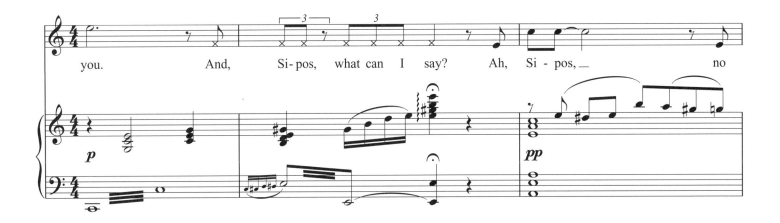

you. And, Si-pos, what can I say? Ah, Si - pos, ___ no

tears, be gay, you know, old friend, I'm in your debt. I

owe you ___ more than I can pos - si - bly re - pay. I won't for -

get.   give your wife a lit-tle kiss   from   Ko-

daly. _____   I nev-er met her but I

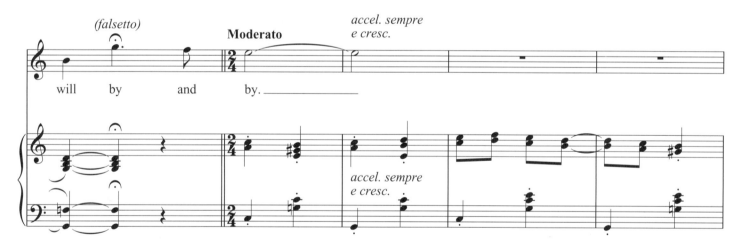

will   by   and   by. _____

Though   I   hate   leav-ing you,

not good- bye. For it's grand know -

-ing you'll all be work - ing for your friend ____

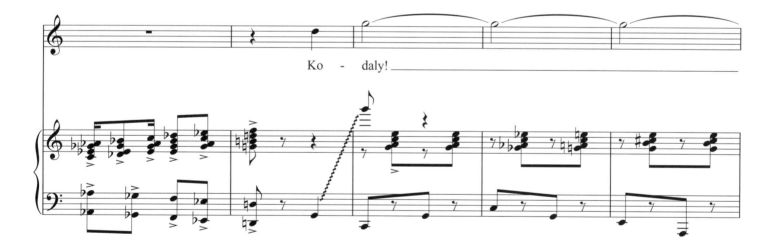

Ko - daly! ____

BRUSH UP YOUR SHAKESPEARE

from *Kiss Me, Kate*

Words and Music by
Cole Porter

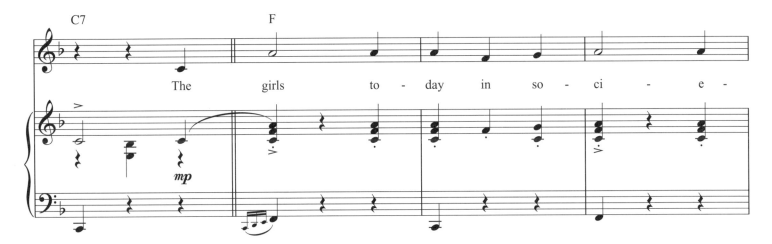

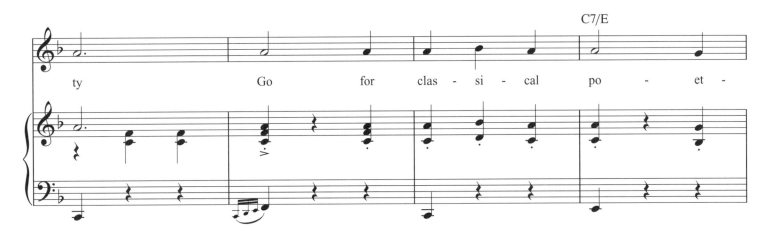

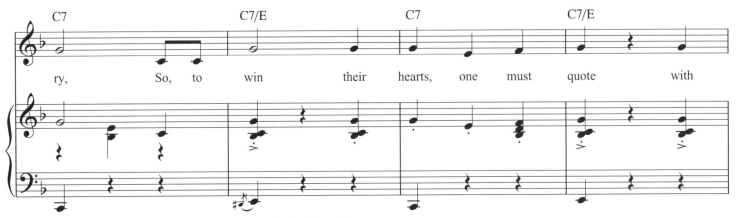

This song is sung by two mobsters, adapted as a solo for this edition.

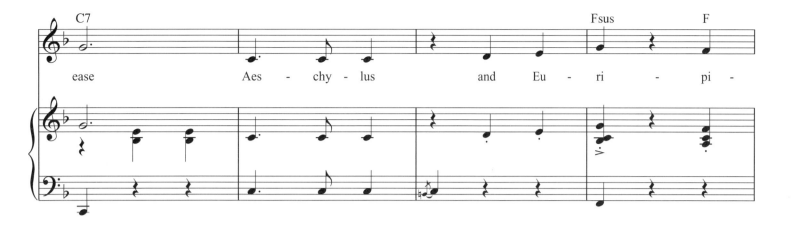

ease   Aes - chy - lus   and   Eu - ri - pi -

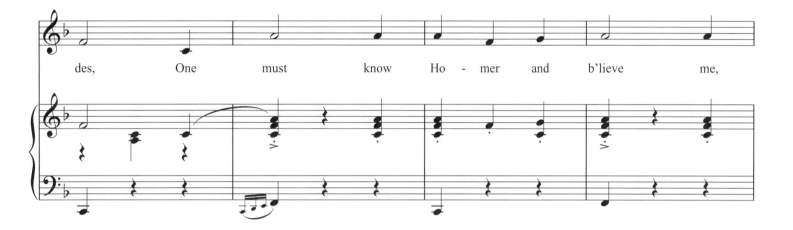

des,   One   must   know   Ho - mer   and   b'lieve   me,

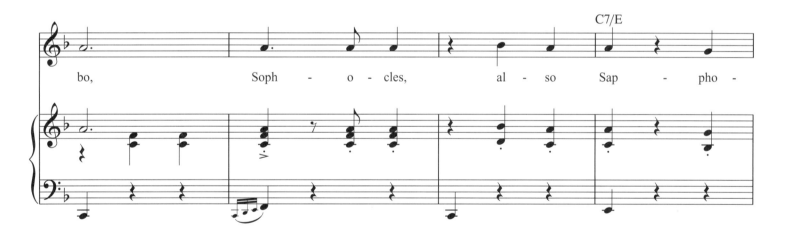

bo,   Soph - o - cles,   al - so   Sap - pho -

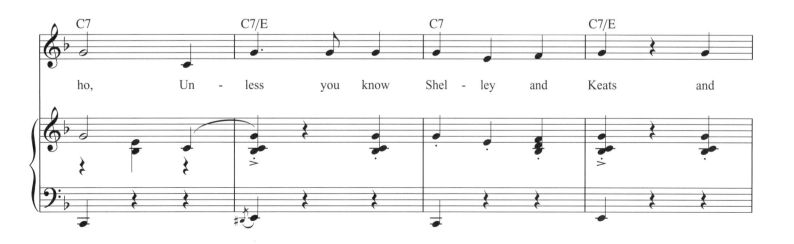

ho,   Un - less   you   know   Shel - ley   and   Keats   and

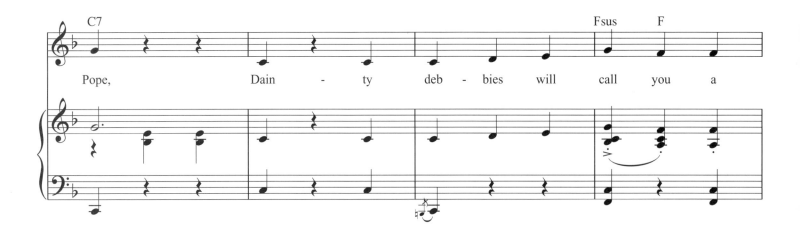

Pope, Dain - ty deb - bies will call you a

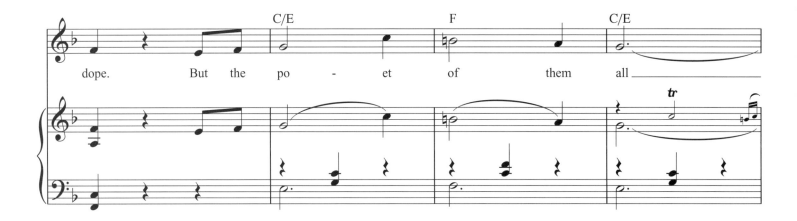

dope. But the po - et of them all _____

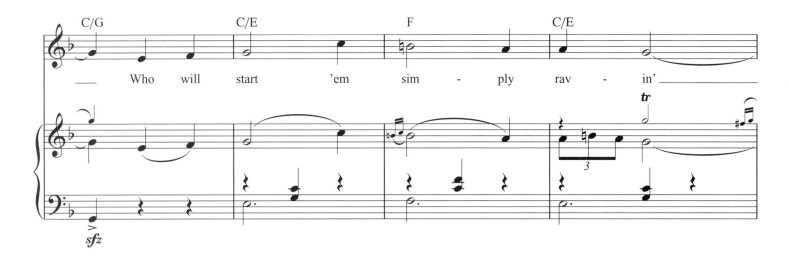

_____ Who will start 'em sim - ply rav - in' _____

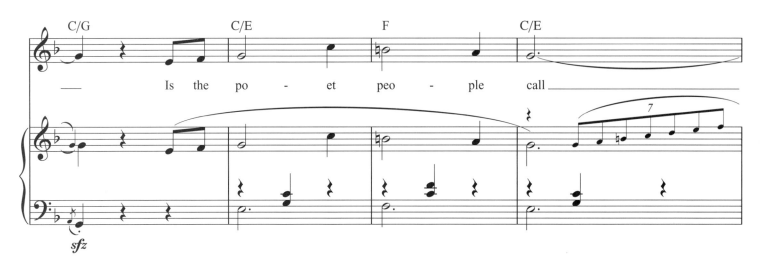

_____ Is the po - et peo - ple call _____

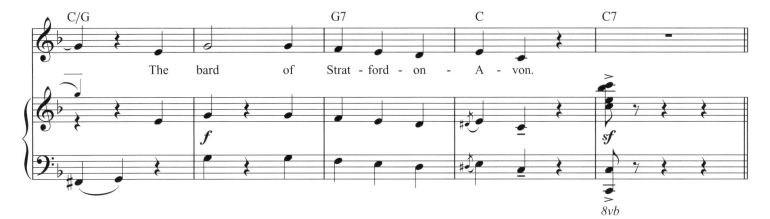

The bard of Strat - ford - on - A - von.

Refrain

Brush up your Shake - speare,
Brush up your Shake - speare,
Brush up your Shake - speare,

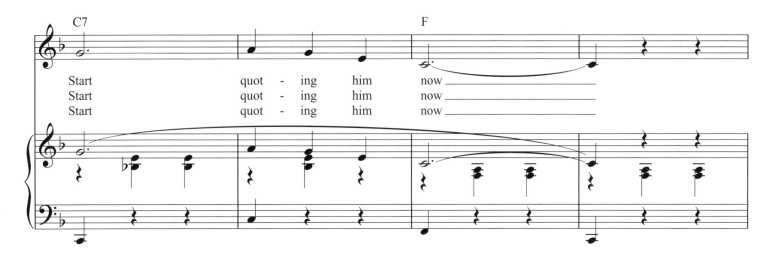

Start quot - ing him now _____
Start quot - ing him now _____
Start quot - ing him _____

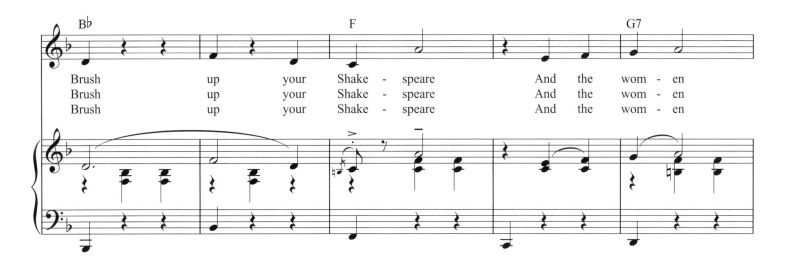

Brush up your Shake - speare And the wom - en
Brush up your Shake - speare And the wom - en
Brush up your Shake - speare And the wom - en

you will wow. Just de - claim a few lines from *O -*
you will wow. If your goil is a Wash - ing - ton
you will wow. If you can't be a ham and do

thel - la And they'll think you're a heck - uv - a fel - la,
Heights dream, Treat the kid to *A Mid - sum - mer Night's Dream,*
Ham - let They will not give a damn or a damn - let.

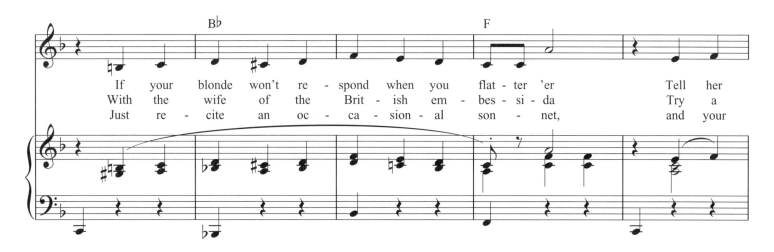

If your blonde won't re - spond when you flat - ter 'er Tell her
With the wife of the Brit - ish em - bes - si - da Try a
Just re - cite an oc - ca - sion - al son - net, and your

what To - ny told Cle - o - pa - ter - er. And if still to be
crack out of *Troi - lus and Cres - si - da,* If she says she won't
lap - 'll have Hon - ey up - on it. When your ba - by is

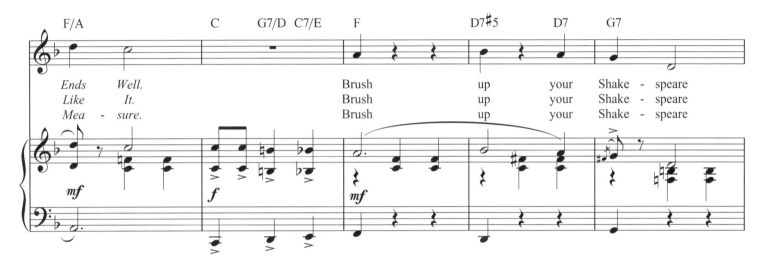

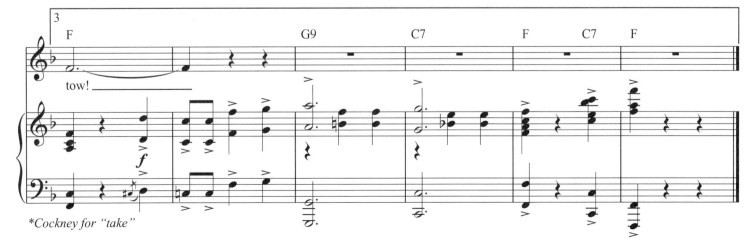

*Cockney for "take"

FRIEND LIKE ME

from *Aladdin*

Music by Alan Menken
Lyrics by Howard Ashman

Bright Two-beat

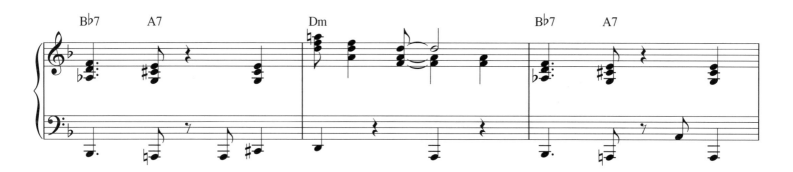

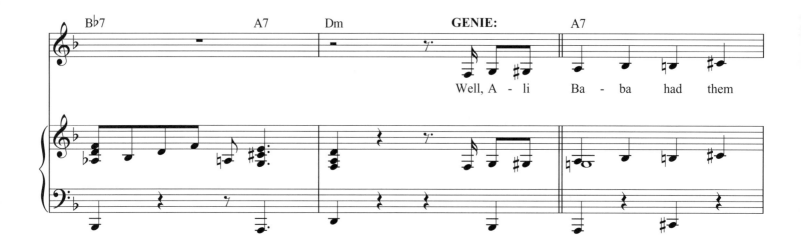

Well, A - li Ba - ba had them

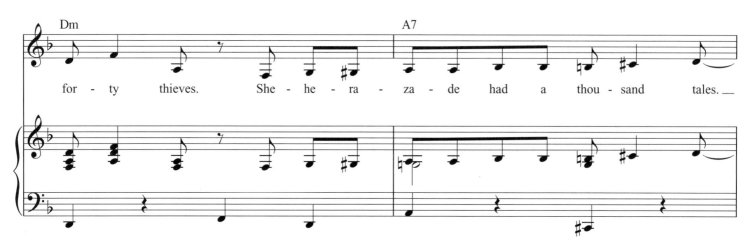

for - ty thieves. She - he - ra - za - de had a thou - sand tales.

But, mas - ter, you in luck 'cause up your sleeves__ you got a

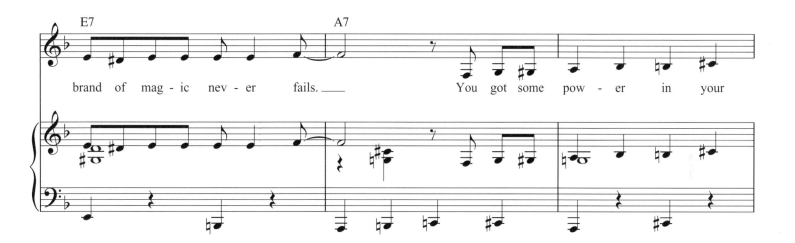

brand of mag - ic nev - er fails.__ You got some pow - er in your

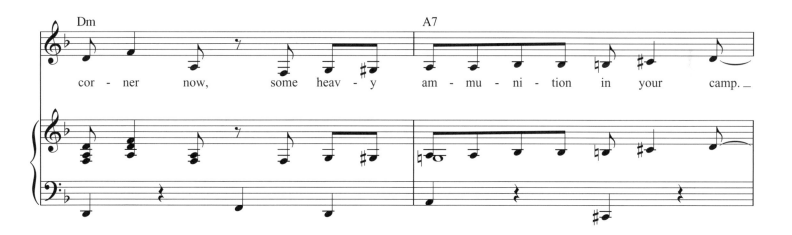

cor - ner now, some heav - y am - mu - ni - tion in your camp.__

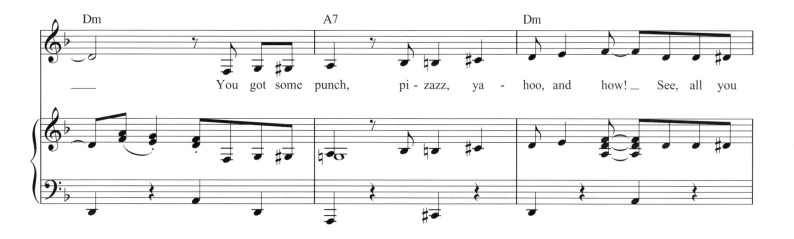

__ You got some punch, pi - zazz, ya - hoo, and how!__ See, all you

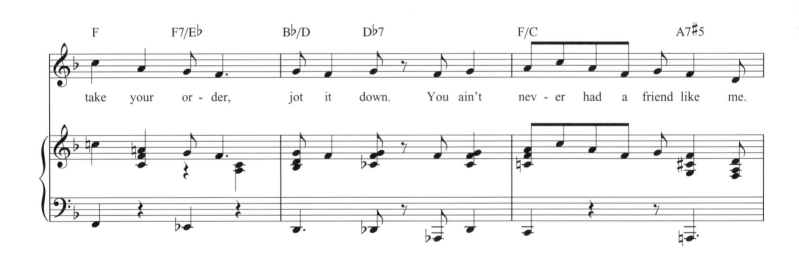

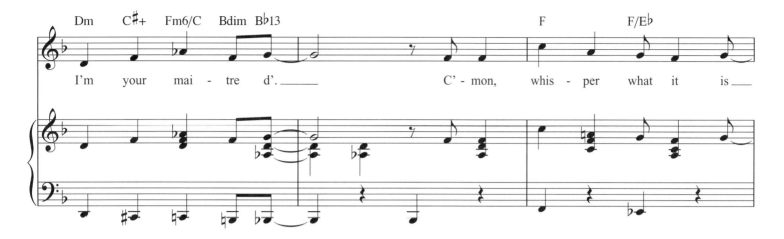

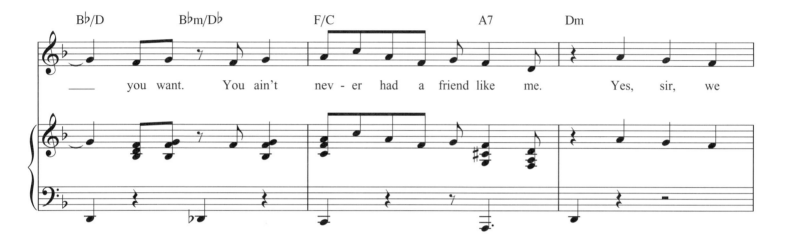

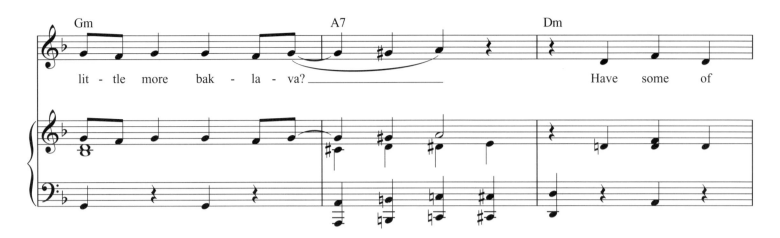

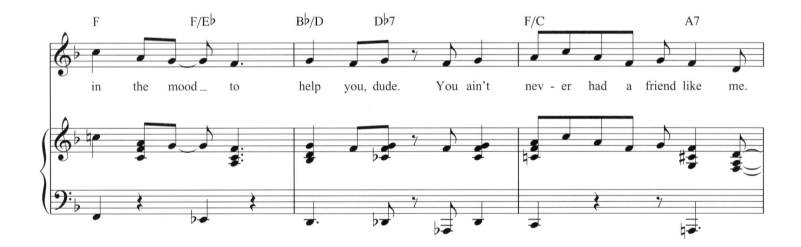

Wa - ah - ah. ___ No, no. ___ Wa - ah - ah. ___

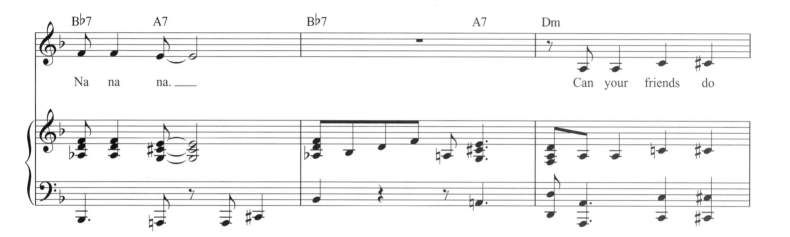

Na na na. ___ Can your friends do

this? Can your friends do that?

Can your friends pull this out their lit - tle hat? ___

Can your friends go poof?

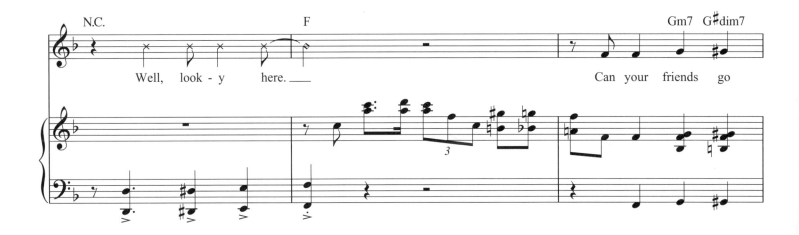

Well, look-y here. ___ Can your friends go

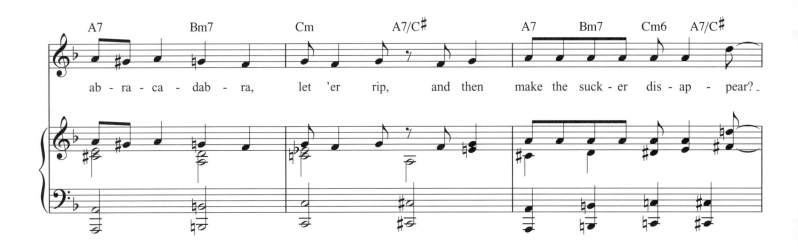

ab - ra - ca - dab - ra, let 'er rip, and then make the suck - er dis - ap - pear? ___

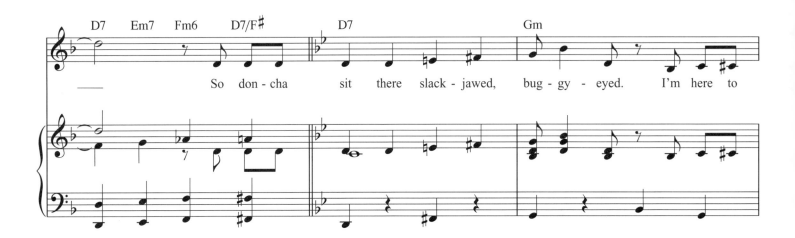

So don - cha sit there slack - jawed, bug - gy - eyed. I'm here to

an-swer all your mid-day prayers. _ You got me bo - na fi - de

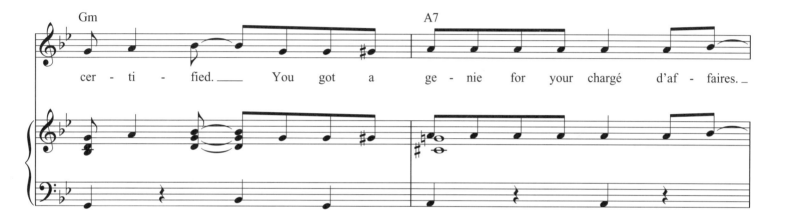

cer - ti - fied. ___ You got a ge - nie for your chargé d'af - faires. _

___ I got a pow - er - ful urge to help you out, so what-cha

wish I real - ly want to know. ___ You got a list that's three miles long, _

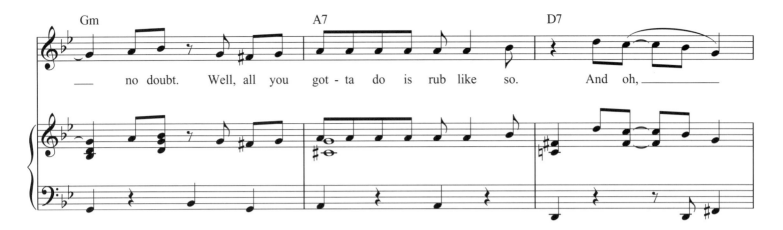

no doubt. Well, all you got-ta do is rub like so. And oh, ____

Mis - ter A - lad - din, sir, ____ have a wish or two or three. ____

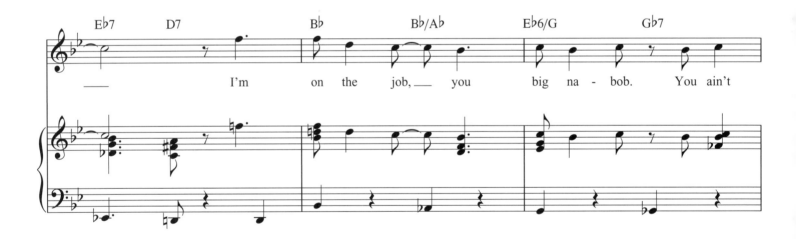

____ I'm on the job, ___ you big na - bob. You ain't

nev - er had a friend, nev - er had a friend, you ain't nev - er had a friend, nev - er

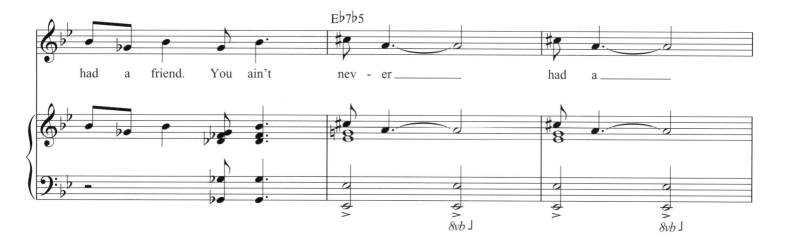

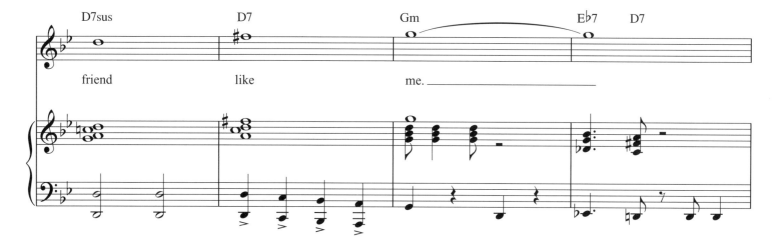

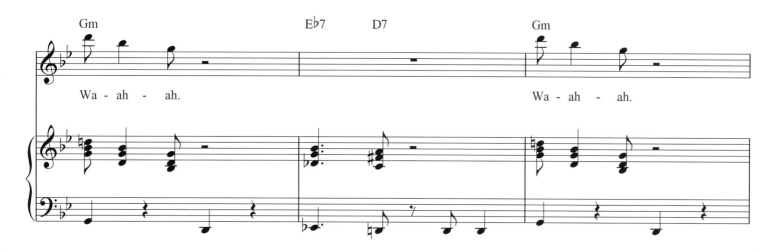

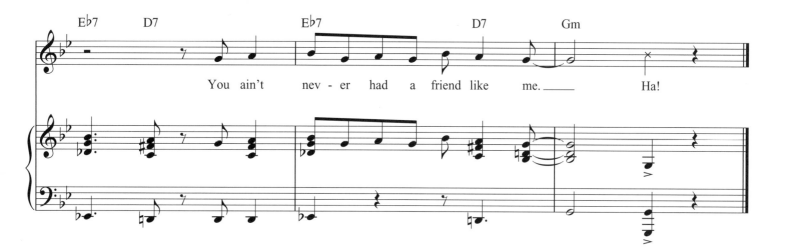

GASTON

from *Beauty and the Beast: The Broadway Musical*

Music by Alan Menken
Lyrics by Howard Ashman

Rowdy barroom Waltz

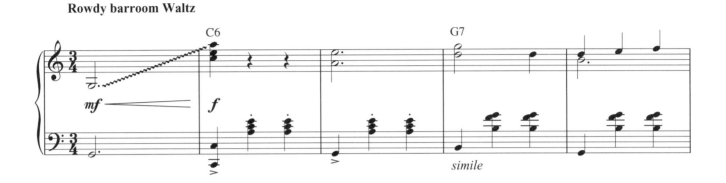

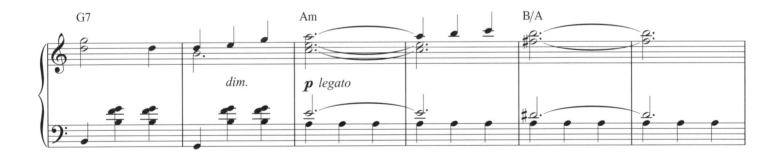

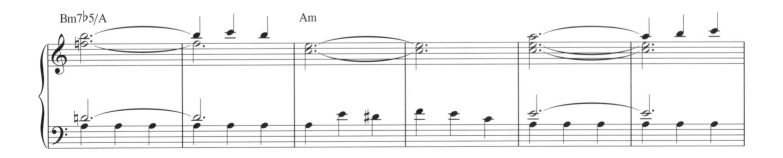

LE FOU: Gosh, it dis - turbs me to see you, Gas - ton, look - ing so

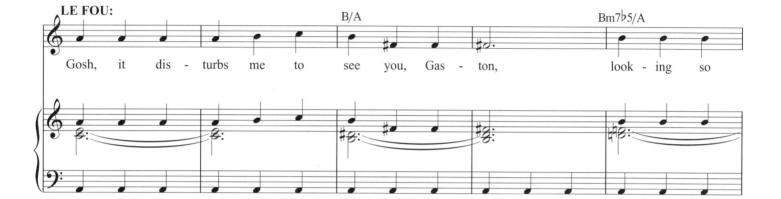

down in the dumps. Ev - 'ry guy here'd like to

be you, Gas - ton, e - ven when tak - ing your lumps.

Le Fou is joined by members of the ensemble, adapted as a solo for this edition.

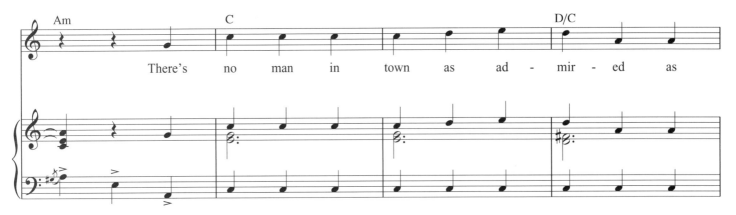

There's no man in town as ad - mir - ed as

you. You're ev - 'ry - one's fa - vor - ite guy.

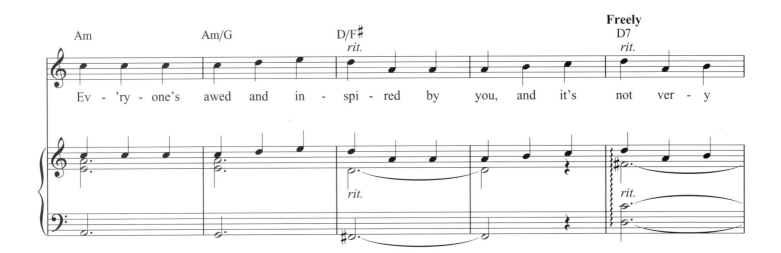

Ev - 'ry - one's awed and in - spi - red by you, and it's not ver - y

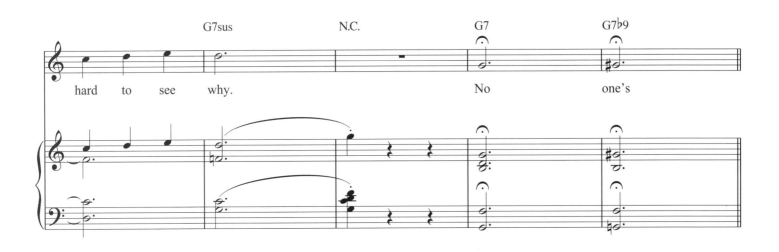

hard to see why. No one's

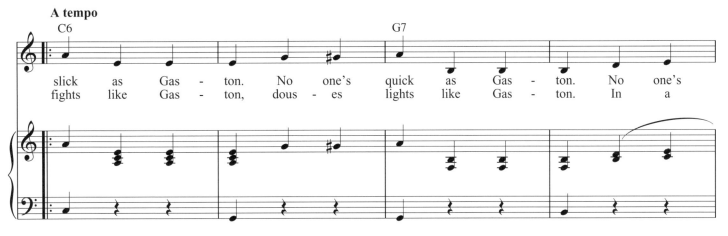

slick as Gas - ton. No one's quick as Gas - ton. No one's
fights like Gas - ton, dous - es lights like Gas - ton. In a

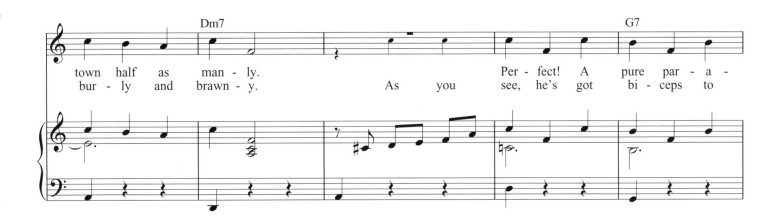

neck's as in - cred - i - bly thick as Gas - ton's. For there's no man in
wrest - ling match, no - bod - y bites like Gas - ton. For there's no one as

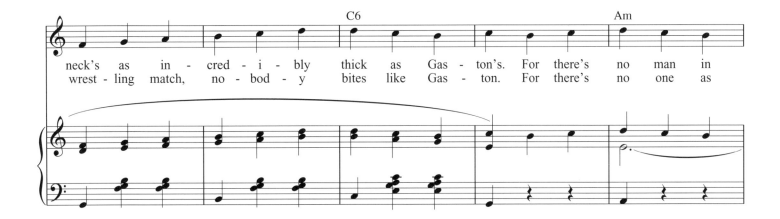

town half as man - ly. Per - fect! A pure par - a -
bur - ly and brawn - y. As you see, he's got bi - ceps to

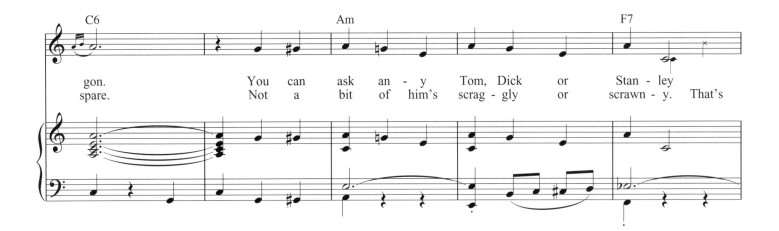

gon. You can ask an - y Tom, Dick or Stan - ley
spare. Not a bit of him's scrag - gly or scrawn - y. That's

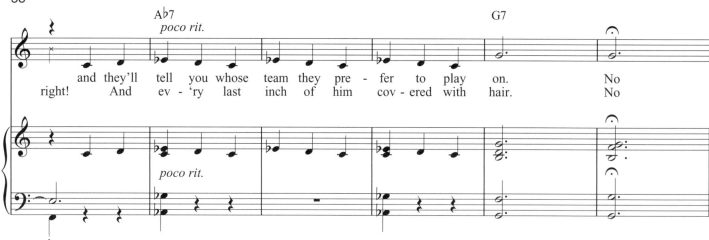

and they'll tell you whose team they pre - fer to play on. No
right! And ev - 'ry last inch of him cov - ered with hair. No

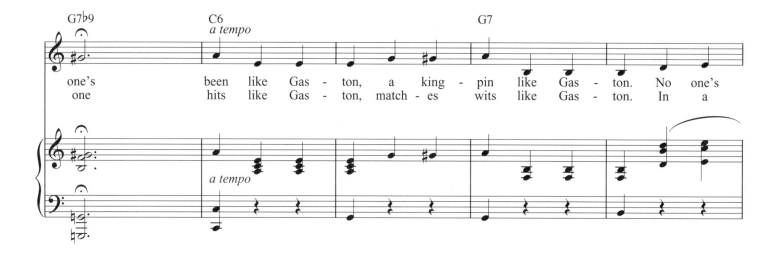

one's been like Gas - ton, a king - pin like Gas - ton. No one's
one hits like Gas - ton, match - es wits like Gas - ton. In a

got a swell cleft in his chin like Gas - ton. As a spec - i - men,
spit - ting match, no - bod - y spits like Gas - ton. He's es - pe - cial - ly

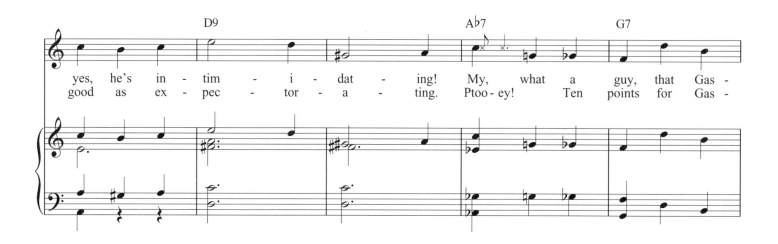

yes, he's in - tim - i - dat - ing! My, what a guy, that Gas -
good as ex - pec - tor - a - ting. Ptoo - ey! Ten points for Gas -

ton! _____ Give five "hur - rahs!" Give twelve "hip -

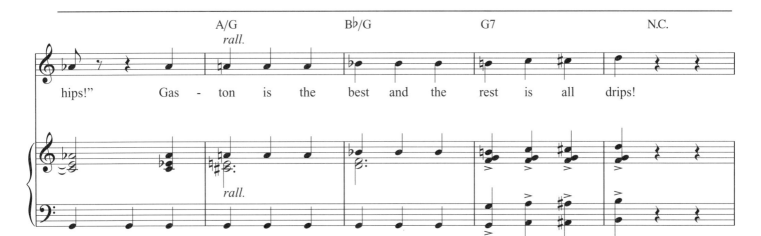

hips!" Gas - ton is the best and the rest is all drips!

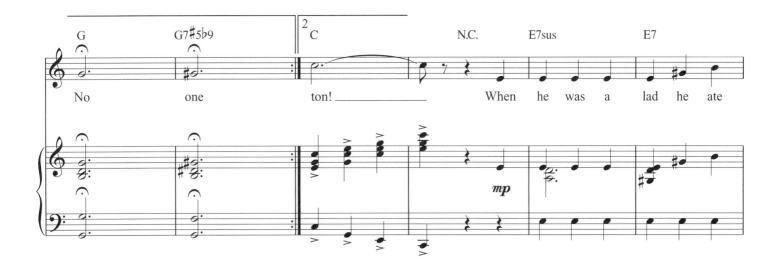

No one ton! _____ When he was a lad he ate

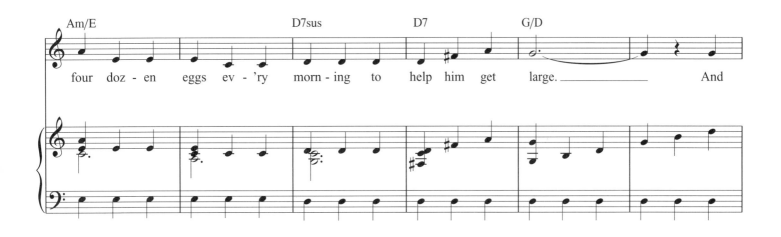

four doz - en eggs ev - 'ry morn - ing to help him get large. _____ And

now that he's grown, he eats five doz - en eggs so he's rough - ly the

size of a barge! No one

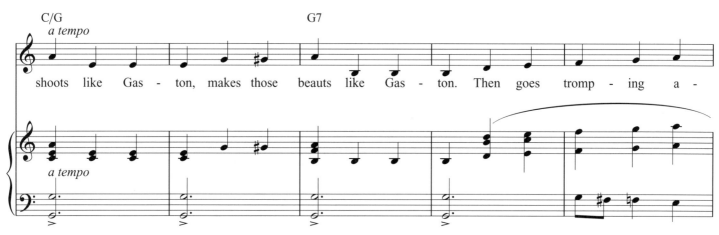

shoots like Gas - ton, makes those beauts like Gas - ton. Then goes tromp - ing a -

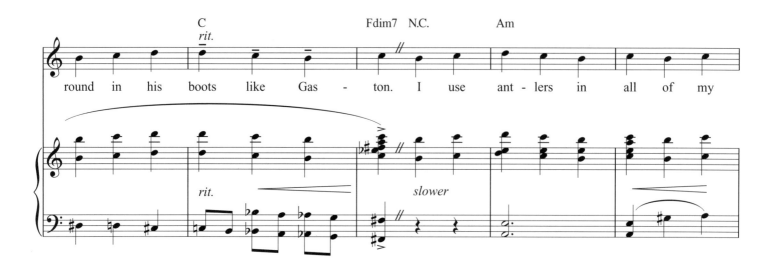

round in his boots like Gas - ton. I use ant - lers in all of my

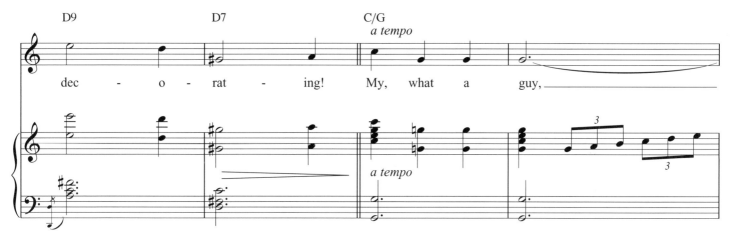

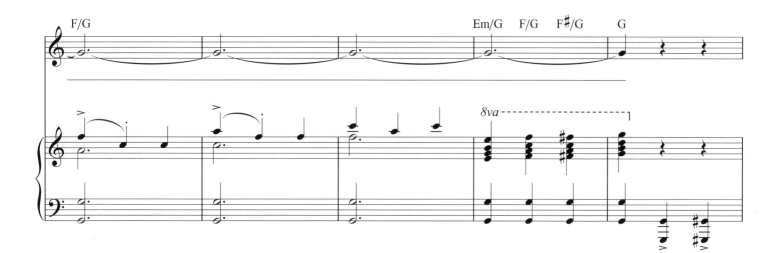

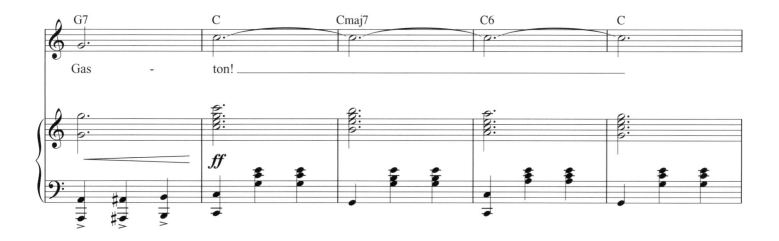

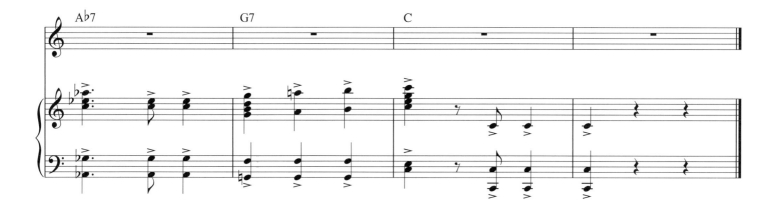

HABEN SIE GEHÖRT DAS DEUTSCHE BAND?

(Have You Ever Heard the German Band?)

from *The Producers*

Music and Lyrics by
Mel Brooks

Bright March, in 2

Ha - ben Sie ge - hört das Deut - sche band? Mit a

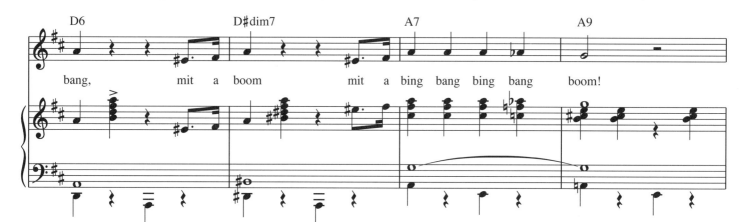

bang, mit a boom mit a bing bang bing bang boom!

Ha - ben Sie ge - hört das Deut - sche band? ____ Mit a

A9#5   D6

bang   mit a boom   mit a bing bang bing bang boom!

Am7   D7   G

Rus - sian folk - songs and French oo - la - la _____

B7   A9/C#   Dm6   B7/D#   E9   G#7   A7

can't com - pare with that Ger - man oom - pah - pah! Ve're say - in'

D   Dmaj7   D6   D   F#m7   B7

Ha - ben Sie ge - hört das Deut - sche band? ____ Mit a

zetz mit a zap mit a zing! _____

Po-lish pol-kas, they're stu-pid und they're rot-ten! It

don't mean a thing if it ain't got that Schwei-gen Rei-gen

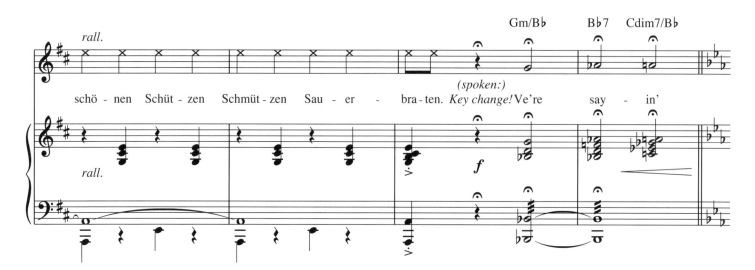

schö-nen Schüt-zen Schmüt-zen Sau-er-bra-ten. *Key change!* Ve're say-in'

(spoken:)

HEIL MYSELF
from *The Producers*

Music and Lyrics by
Mel Brooks

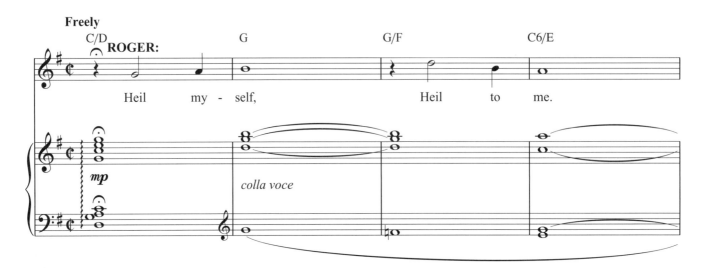

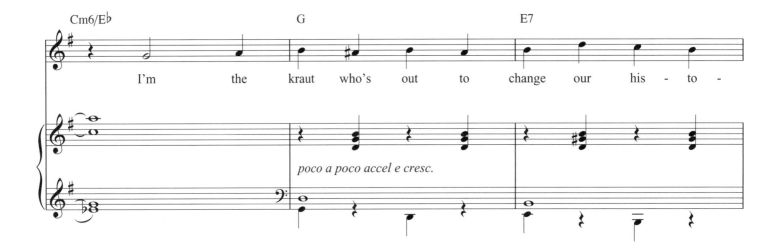

Roger is joined by ensemble in this production number, adapted as a solo here.

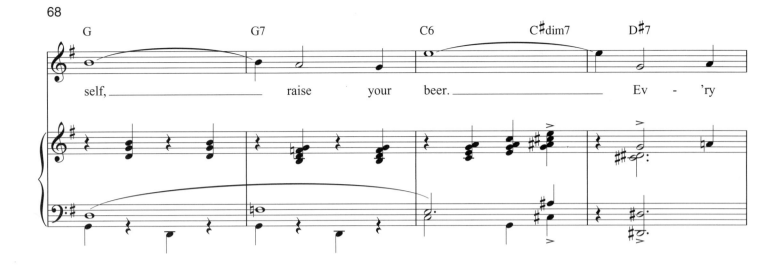

self, _____ raise your beer. _____ Ev - 'ry

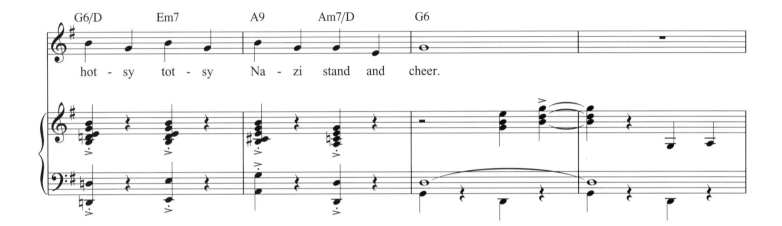

hot - sy tot - sy Na - zi stand and cheer.

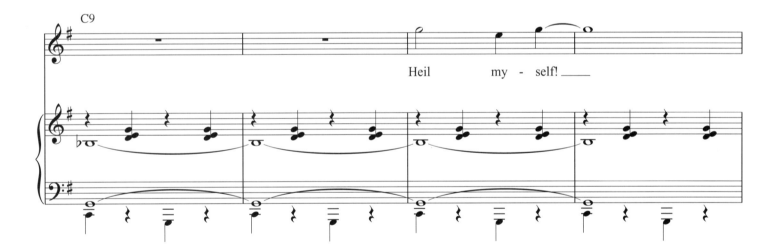

Heil my - self! ____

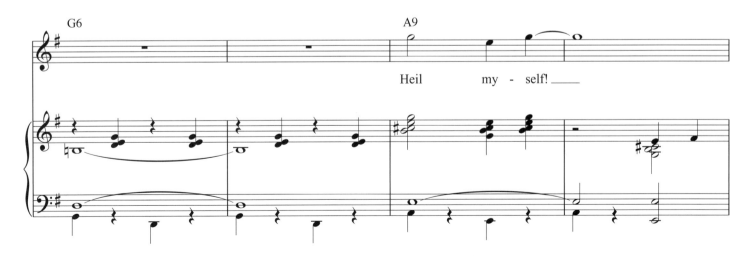

Heil my - self! ____

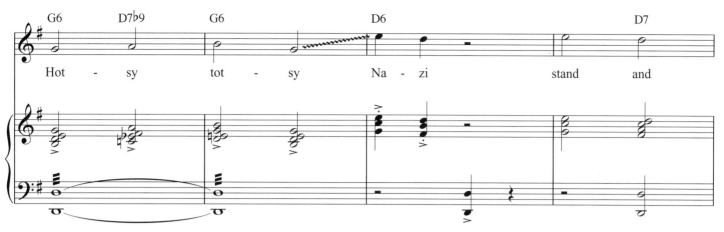

Hot- sy tot- sy Na - zi stand and

cheer. _____

The

Füh - rer _____ is caus - ing _____ a

Make a great big smile! Ev-'ry-one sieg heil to me, _____ won-der-ful me! _____

I AM ALDOLPHO
from *The Drowsy Chaperone*

Words and Music by Lisa Lambert
and Greg Morrison

Bright Paso Doble

ALDOLPHO:

I'm

A Tempo (tango, in 4)

sure that you have heard the name Al - dol - pho,   a   lad - ies' man who wins ac - claim, Al -

peat my-self,　　I am Al-dol-pho.　　　I can sing it high: Al-dol-pho.

Freely

I can sing it low: Al-dol-pho. I can sing it ver-y fast: Al-dol-pho.　I can sing it ver-y slow...

ly　*I'd do it now, but it would take*
hours. Now let us see if you
can remember my name.　　Now　who's the fel-low that you see? Al-

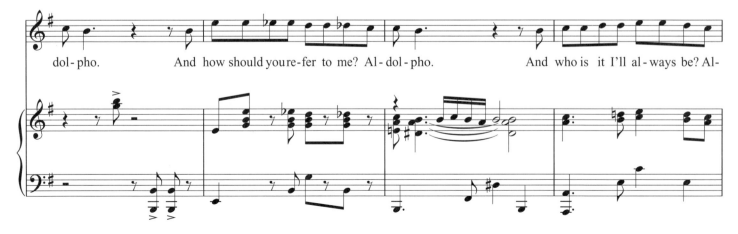

dol-pho.　　And how should you re-fer to me? Al-dol-pho.　　And who is it I'll al-ways be? Al-

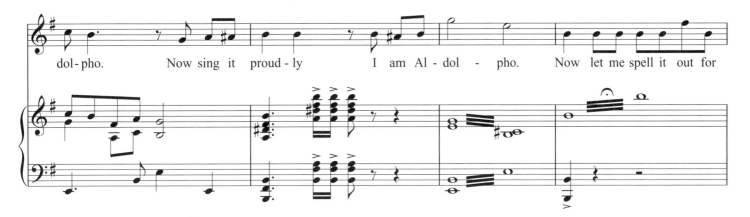

dol-pho. Now sing it proud - ly I am Al - dol - pho. Now let me spell it out for

you *for all you lovely ladies who didn't hear,*
for some reason maybe you are hard of
hearing or something - I don't know. It goes

a - a - a - a - a - a - al

[colla voce]

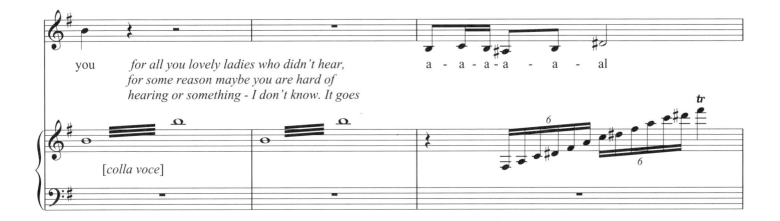

do - ho - ho - ho - ho - hol f - f - f - f - f - fo I am Al - dol - pho _____

ff

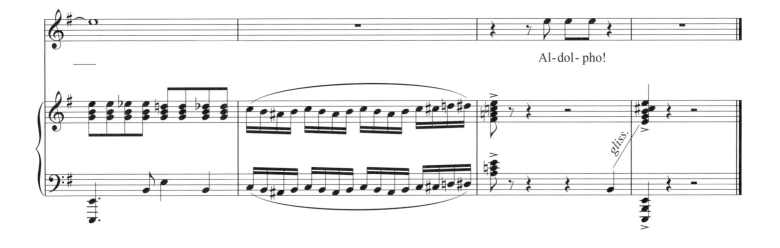

Al - dol - pho!

gliss.

I'M CALM

from *A Funny Thing Happened on the Way to the Forum*

Words and Music by
Stephen Sondheim

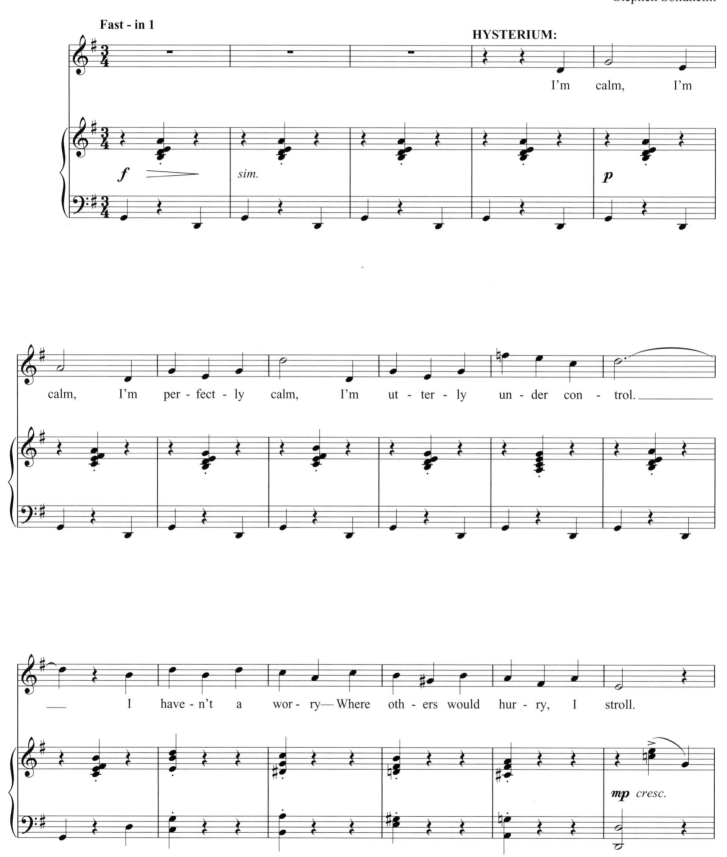

Slower - In 3

slowly

I must think calm com - fort - ing

things: But - ter - fly wings, Em - er - ald rings.

Or a mur - mur - ing brook—

rit.

Mur - mur - ing, mur - mur - ing, mur - mur - ing— Look: I'm calm, I'm

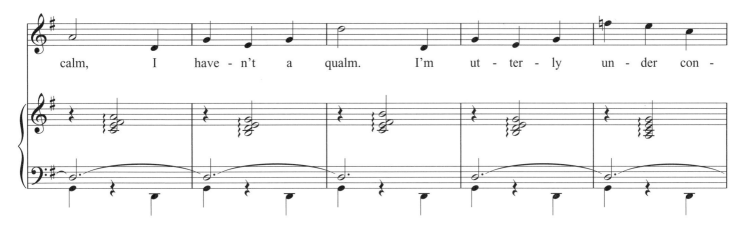

calm, I have -n't a qualm. I'm ut -ter -ly un -der con -

Rubato [*He yawns*]

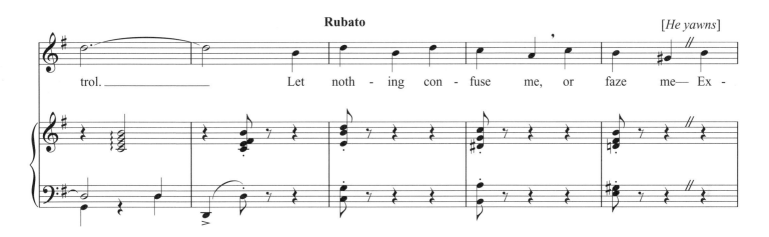

trol. _____ Let noth -ing con -fuse me, or faze me— Ex -

Slowly

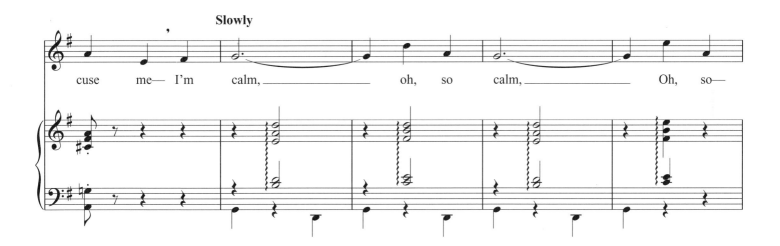

cuse me— I'm calm, _____ oh, so calm, _____ Oh, so—

(*He SCREAMS*) **Presto**

I'M NOT WEARING UNDERWEAR TODAY
from the Broadway Musical *Avenue Q*

Music and Lyrics by Robert Lopez
and Jeff Marx

Fast and circus-like

BRIAN:

I'm not wear-ing un-der-wear to-day! No, I'm not wear-ing un-der-wear to-day!

not that you prob - 'ly care much a - bout my un - der - wear,

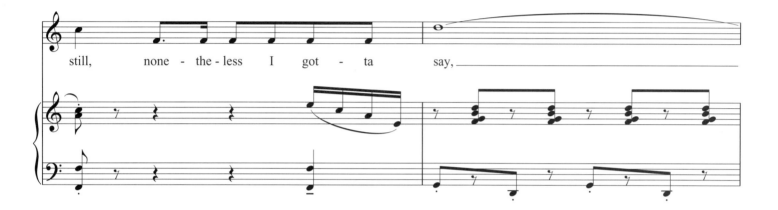

still, none - the - less I got - ta say, _____

that I'm not wear - ing

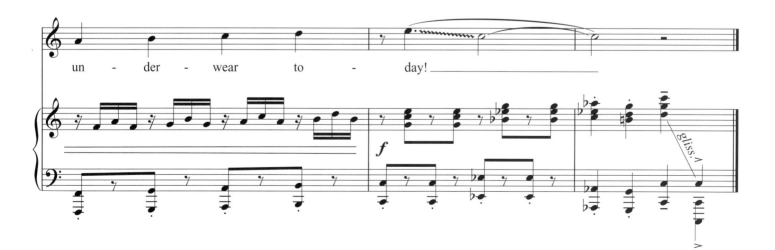

un - der - wear to - day!

IF I WERE KING OF THE FOREST
from *The Wizard of Oz*

Lyric by E.Y. Harburg
Music by Harold Arlen

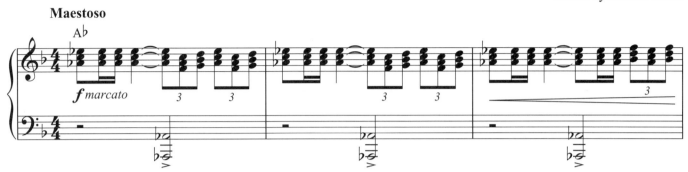

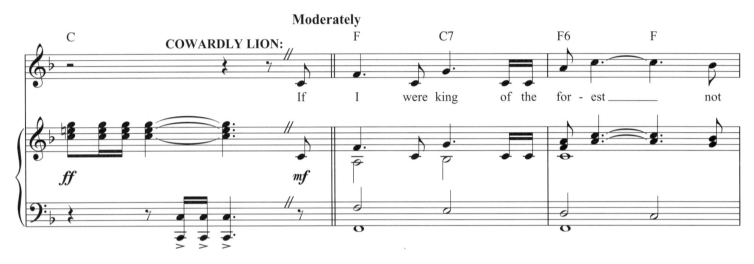

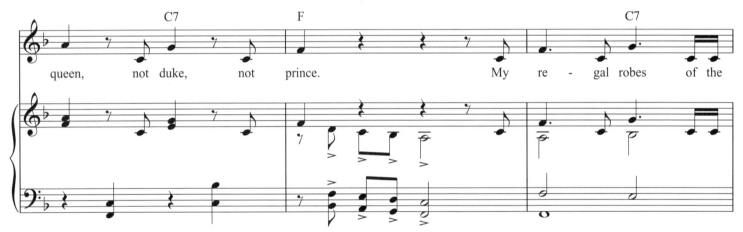

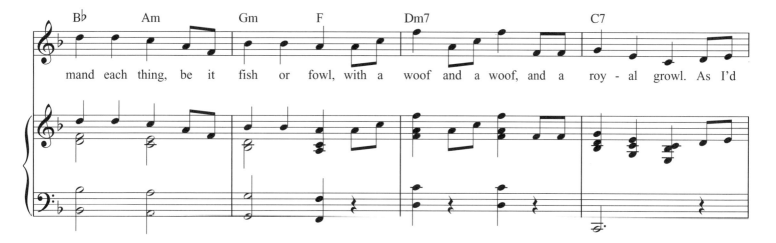

mand each thing, be it fish or fowl, with a woof and a woof, and a roy - al growl. As I'd

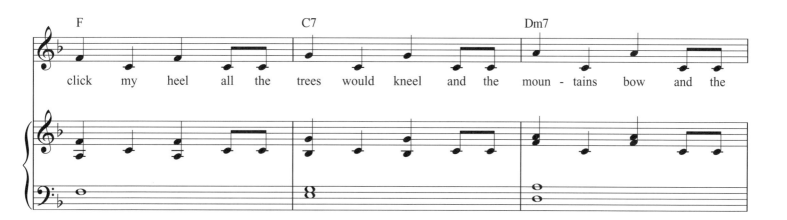

click my heel all the trees would kneel and the moun - tains bow and the

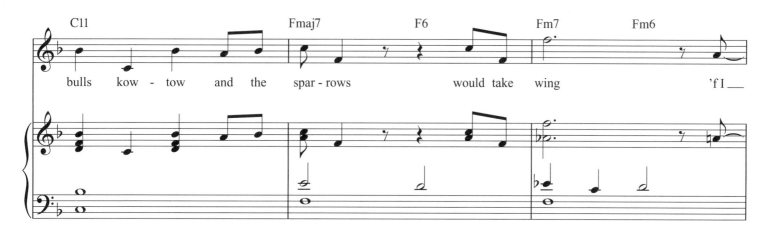

bulls kow - tow and the spar - rows would take wing 'f I ___

___ 'f I ___ were king. ___

IN OLD BAVARIA
from *The Producers*

Music and Lyrics by
Mel Brooks

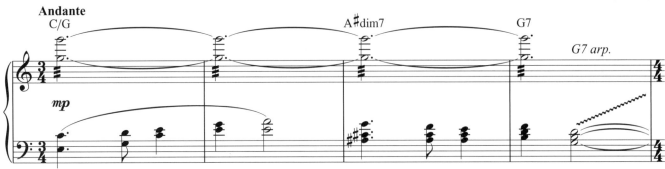

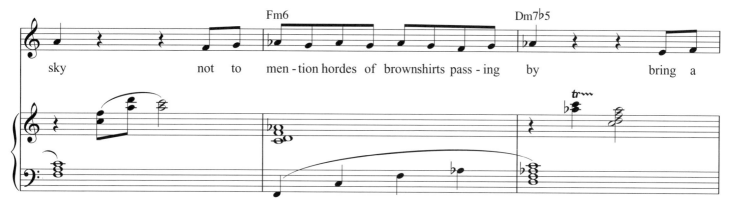

sky   not to men - tion hordes of brownshirts pass - ing   by   bring a

tear to ev - 'ry sin - gle Na - zi eye   in

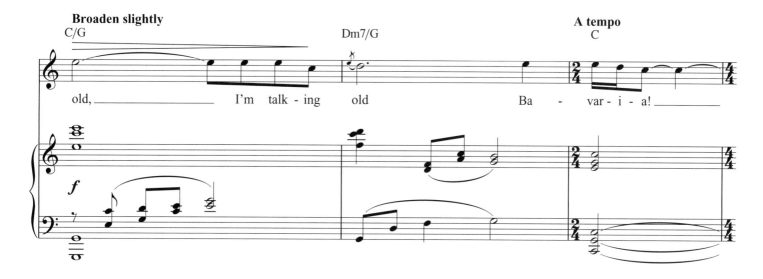

Broaden slightly   **A tempo**

old, _____ I'm talk - ing old   Ba - var - i - a! _____

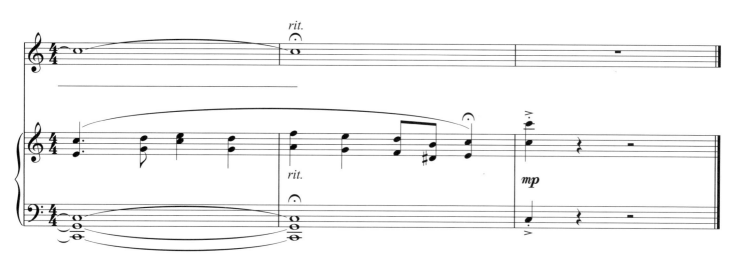

IT AIN'T NECESSARILY SO

from *Porgy and Bess*

Music and Lyrics by George Gershwin,
DuBose and Dorothy Heyward
and Ira Gershwin

Moderately, with humor

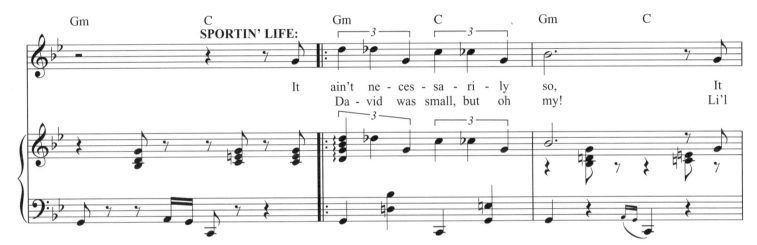

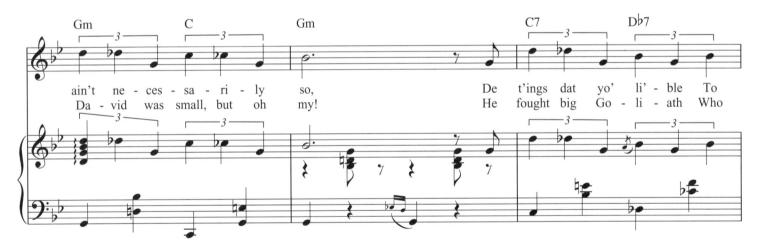

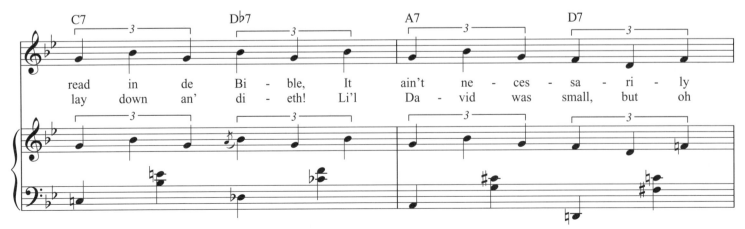

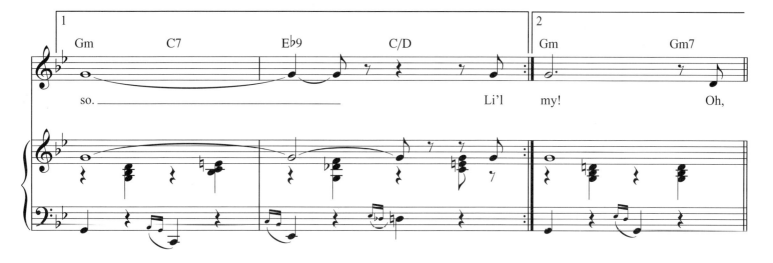

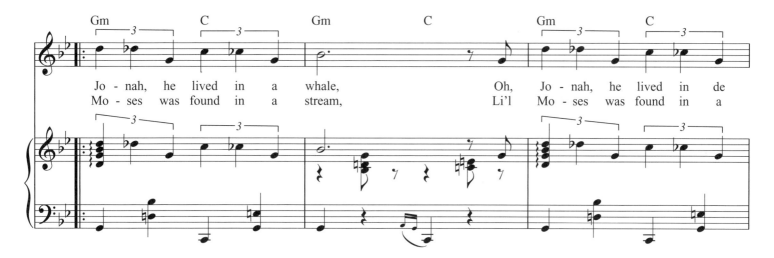

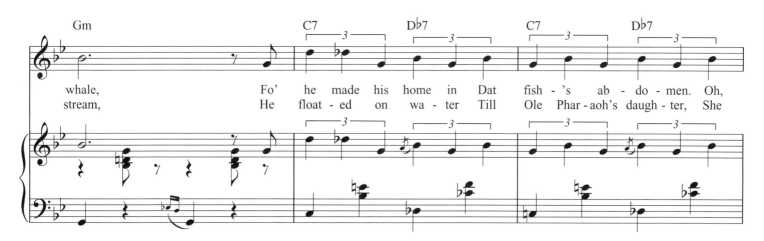

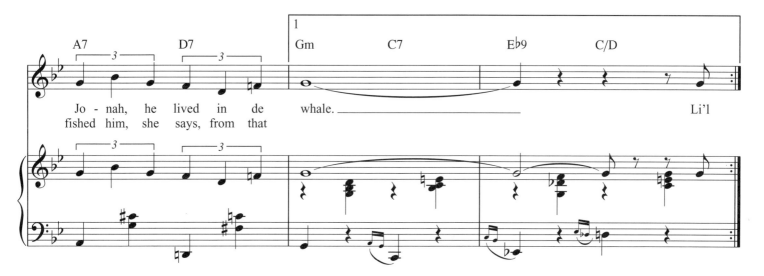

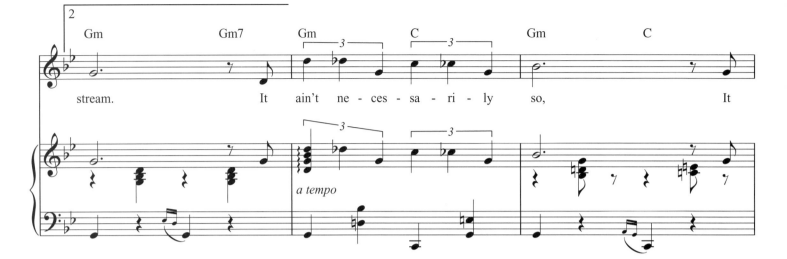

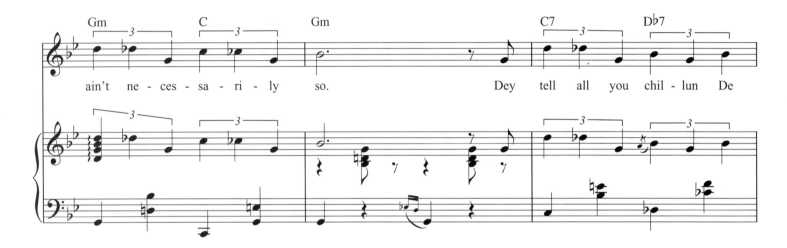

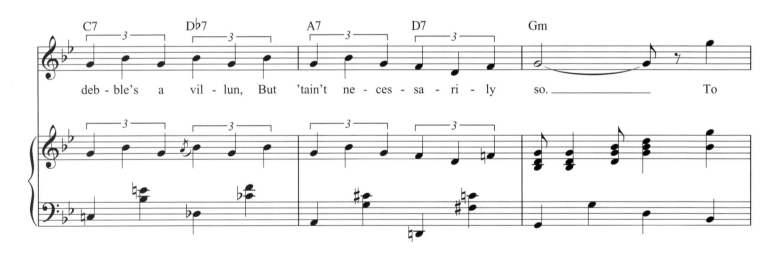

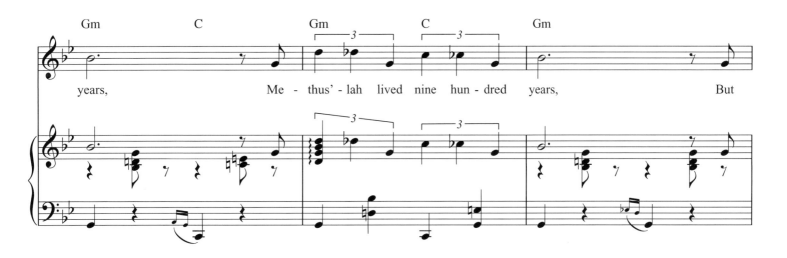

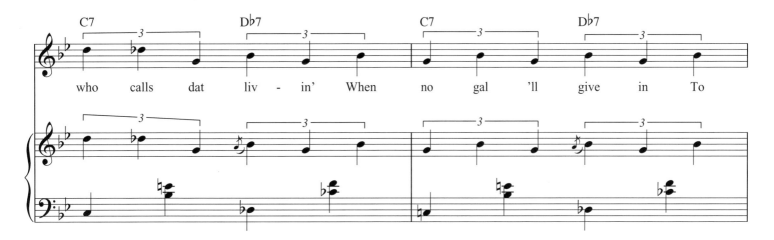

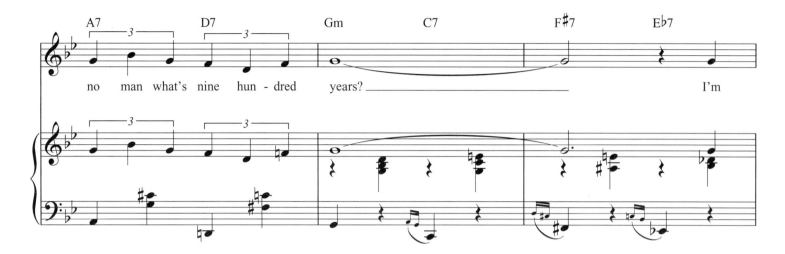

no man what's nine hun - dred years? _____ I'm

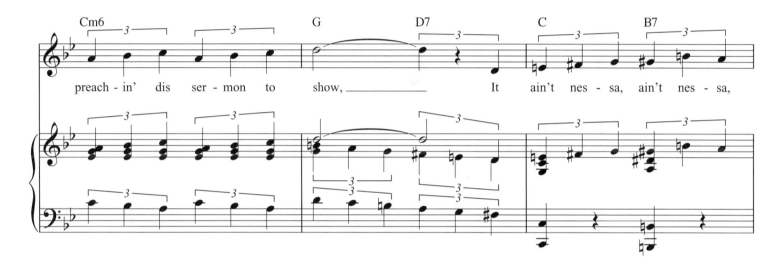

preach - in' dis ser - mon to show, _____ It ain't nes - sa, ain't nes - sa,

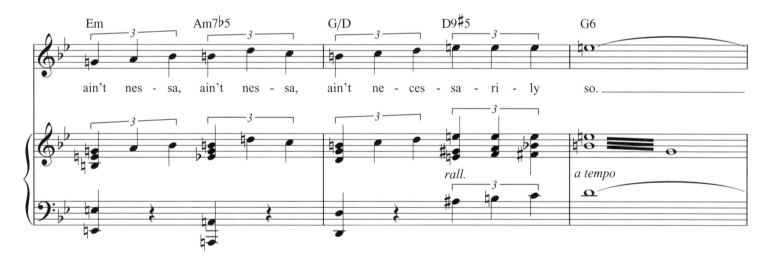

ain't nes - sa, ain't nes - sa, ain't ne - ces - sa - ri - ly so. _____

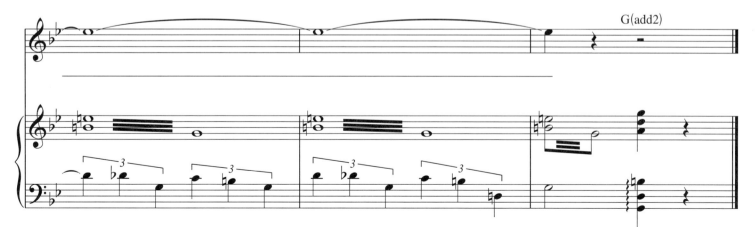

IF YOU WERE GAY
from the Broadway Musical *Avenue Q*

Music and Lyrics by Robert Lopez
and Jeff Marx

free to __ say that I was gay! (But I'm not gay!)

If you were

queer, I'd still be here, year af - ter

year, be - cause you're dear to __ me. And I know that

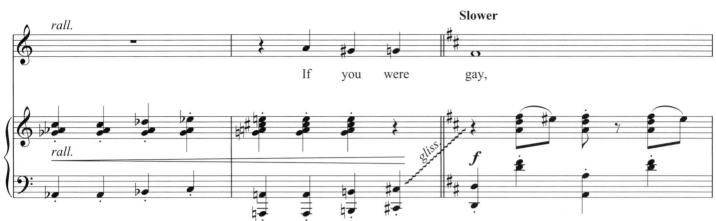

be   be - side you ev - 'ry___ day,

to tell you it's o - kay,   You were just born that __ way,

And as they say: It's in your D - N - A, you're

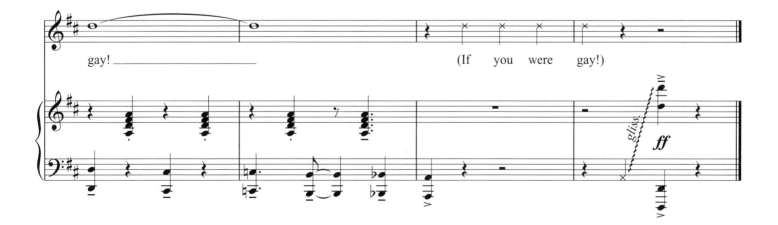

gay! _____   (If you were gay!)

LADIES IN THEIR SENSITIVITIES

from *Sweeney Todd*

Words and Music by
Stephen Sondheim

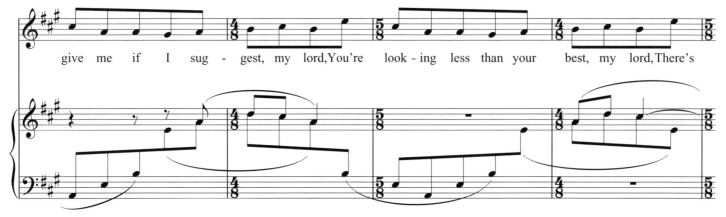

powder up-on your vest, my lord, And stub-ble up-on your cheek.

And la-dies, my lord, are weak.

Larghetto (♩ = 80)
(Wincing delicately)

poco rubato

sempre **mp**

La-dies in their sen-si-tiv-i-ties, my lord, Have a frag-ile sen-si-

bil-i-ty. When a girl's e-mer-gent, Prob-ab-ly it's ur-gent

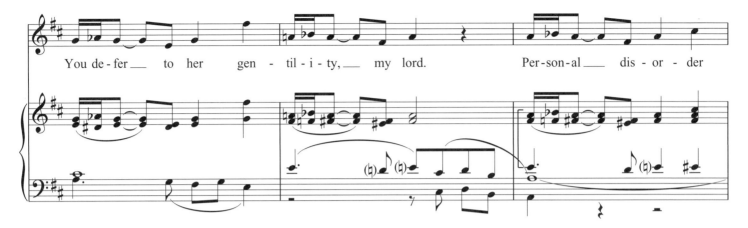

You de-fer ___ to her gen - til - i - ty, ___ my lord. Per-son-al ___ dis - or - der

can not be ___ ig-nored, Giv-en their ___ gen - teel pro - cliv - i - ties. ___

Mean ing no ___ of-fense, it hap-pens they ___ re-sents it, La - dies in ___ their sen - si -

Tempo primo

tiv - i - ties, ___ my lord. Fret not, though, my lord, I know a place, my lord, A

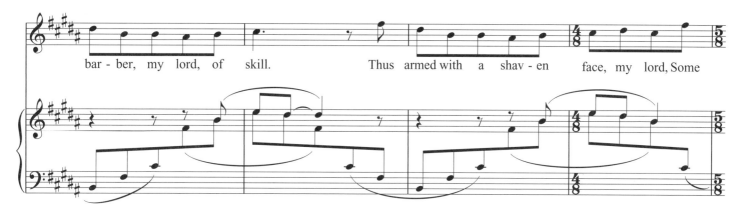

barber, my lord, of skill. Thus armed with a shav-en face, my lord, Some

eau de co-logne to brace my lord, And musk to en-hance the chase, my lord, You'll

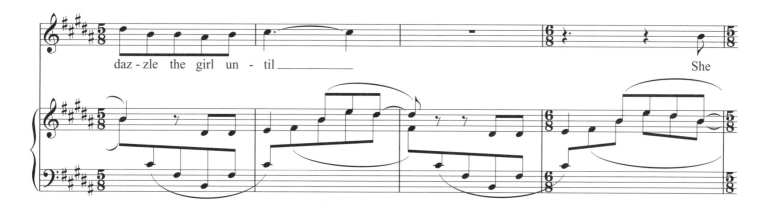

daz-zle the girl un-til_____ She

bows to your ev-'ry will.____

LES POISSONS

from *The Little Mermaid – A Broadway Musical*

Music by Alan Menken
Lyrics by Howard Ashman

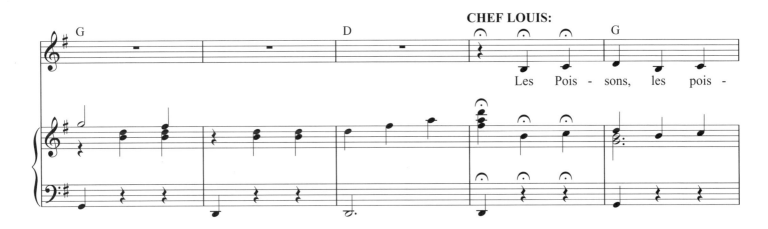

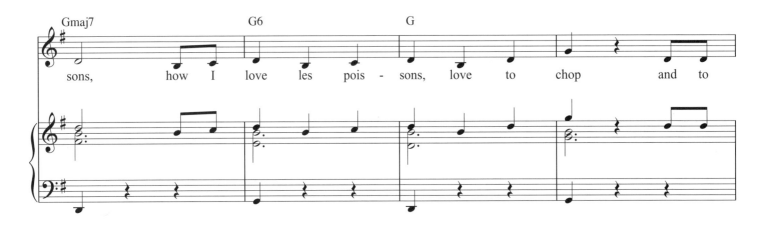

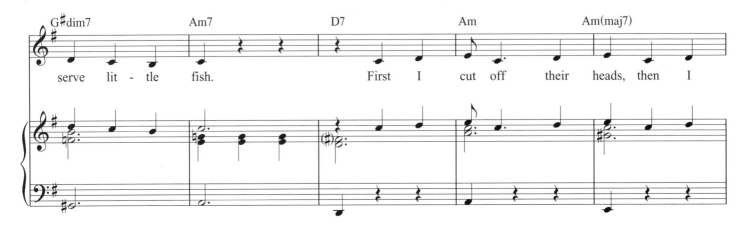

pull out their bones. Ah mais oui, ca c'est tou - jours de - lish.

Les pois - sons, les pois - sons, hee hee hee, ____ hah hah hah. ____

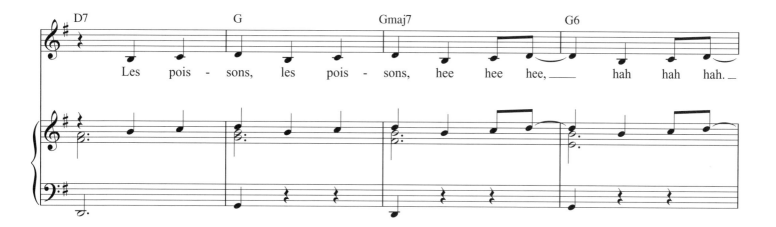

____ With the cleav - er I hack them in two. I pull

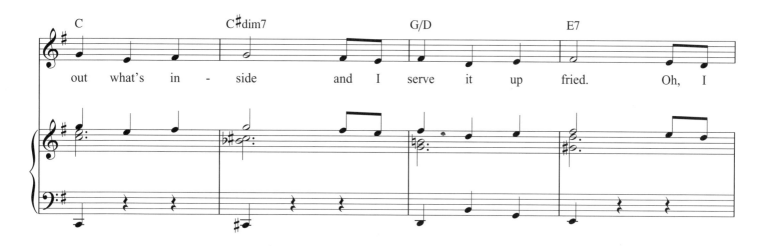

out what's in - side and I serve it up fried. Oh, I

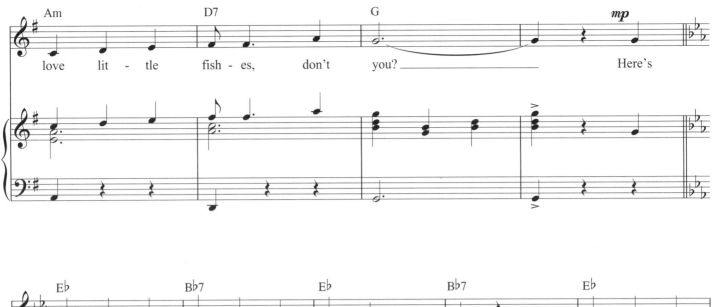

love lit - tle fish - es, don't you?_____ Here's

some - thing for tempt - ing the pal - ate,_____ Pre - pared in the

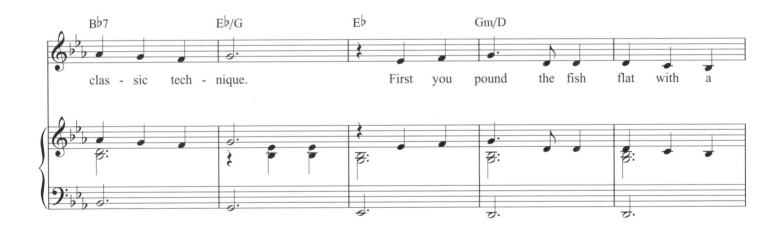

clas - sic tech - nique. First you pound the fish flat with a

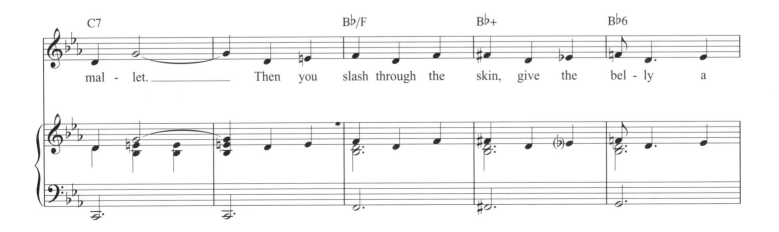

mal - let._____ Then you slash through the skin, give the bel - ly a

slice, then you rub some salt in 'cause that makes it taste

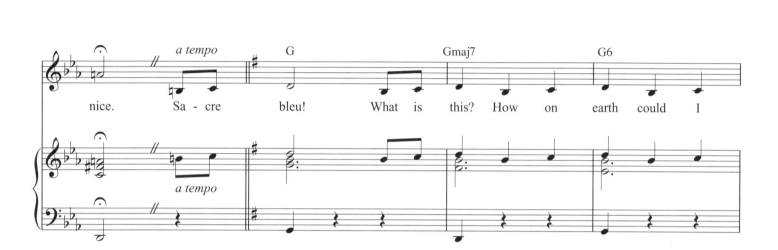

nice. Sa - cre bleu! What is this? How on earth could I

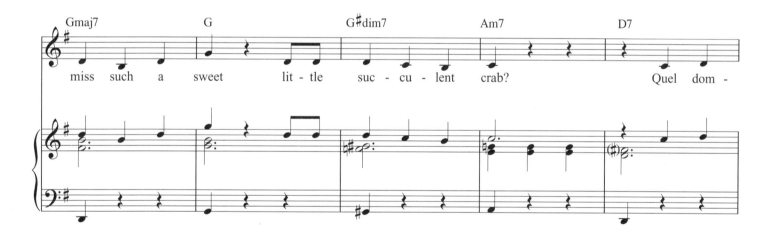

miss such a sweet lit - tle suc - cu - lent crab? Quel dom -

mage. What a loss. Here we go in the sauce. Now some

flour ___ I think, just a dab. Now I stuff you with

bread. It don't hurt 'cause you're dead. And you're cer - tain - ly luck - y you

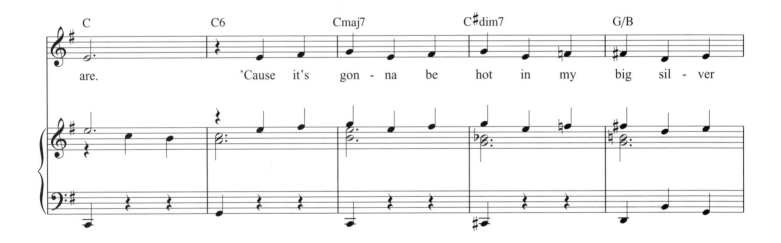

are. 'Cause it's gon - na be hot in my big sil - ver

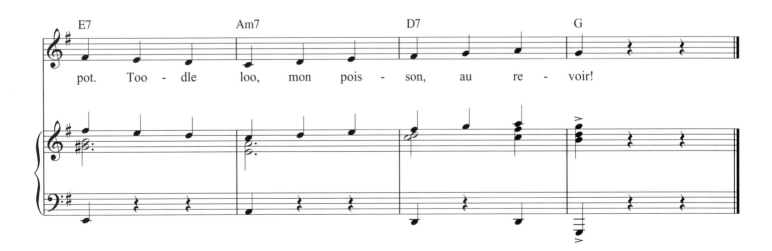

pot. Too - dle loo, mon pois - son, au re - voir!

ME
from *Beauty and the Beast: The Broadway Musical*

Music by Alan Menken
Lyrics by Tim Rice

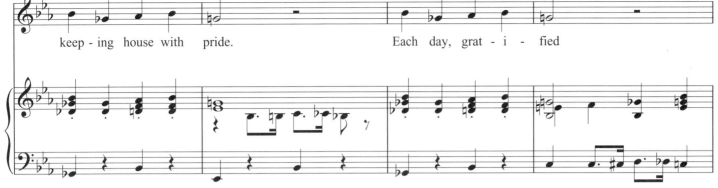

keep - ing house with pride. Each day, grat - i - fied

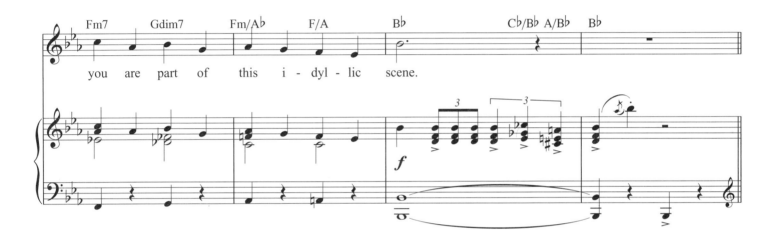

you are part of this i - dyl - lic scene.

(Spoken:) Picture this: A rustic hunting lodge... my latest kill, roasting over the fire... my little wife massaging my feet...

while the little ones play on the floor with the dogs. Oh, we'll have six or seven!

108

lead to... The best things in life are... All's well that ends with

me! _____ Es - cape me? There's no way. Cer - tain as

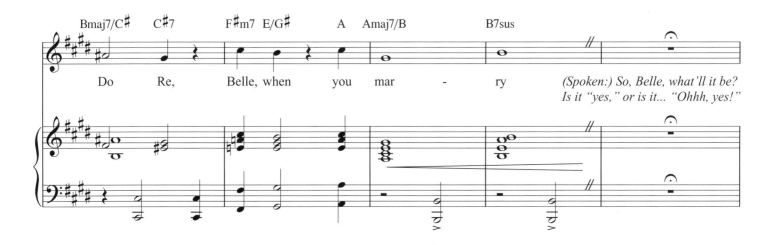

Do Re, Belle, when you mar - ry (Spoken:) So, Belle, what'll it be?
Is it "yes," or is it... "Ohhh, yes!"

me! _____

MISTER CELLOPHANE

from *Chicago*

Words by Fred Ebb
Music by John Kander

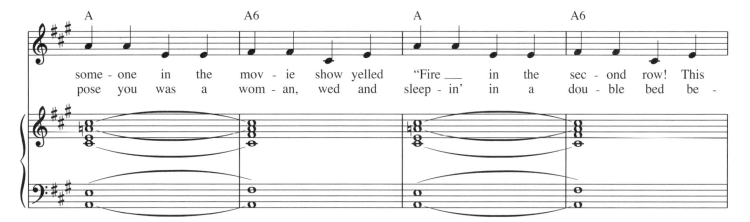

some - one in the mov - ie show yelled "Fire ___ in the sec - ond row! This
pose you was a wom - an, wed and sleep - in' in a dou - ble bed be -

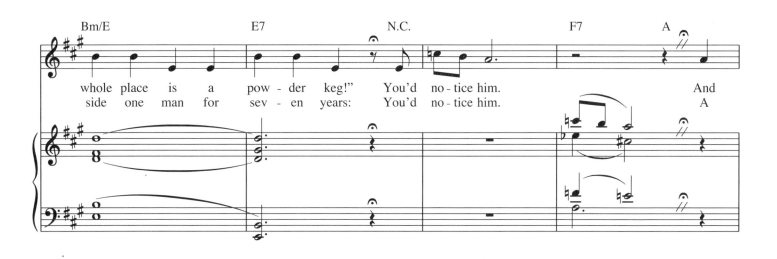

whole place is a pow - der keg!" You'd no - tice him. And
side one man for sev - en years: You'd no - tice him. A

e - ven with-out cluck-ing like a hen, ev - 'ry-one gets no - ticed now and
hu - man be-ing's made of more than air. With all that bulk you're bound to see him

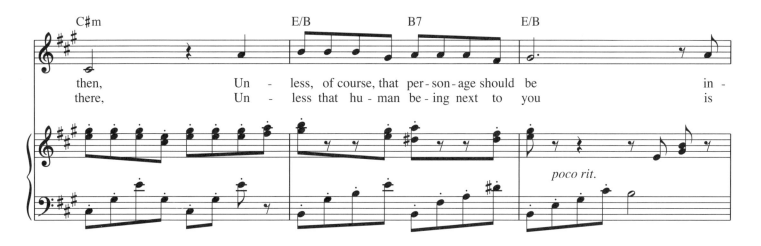

then, Un - less, of course, that per-son-age should be in -
there, Un - less that hu - man be-ing next to you is

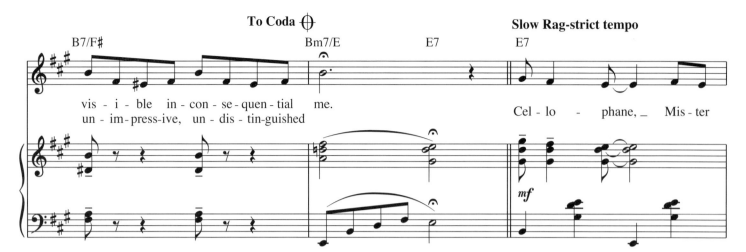

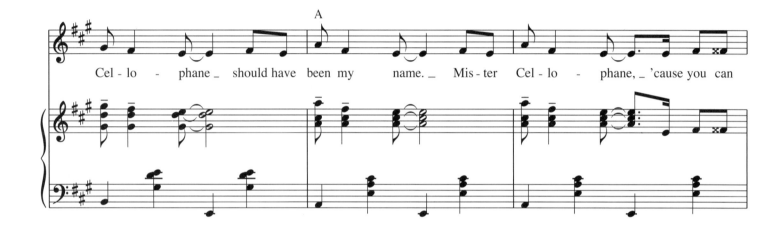

been my name, _ Mis-ter Cel-lo-phane, _ 'cause you can see right thru me,

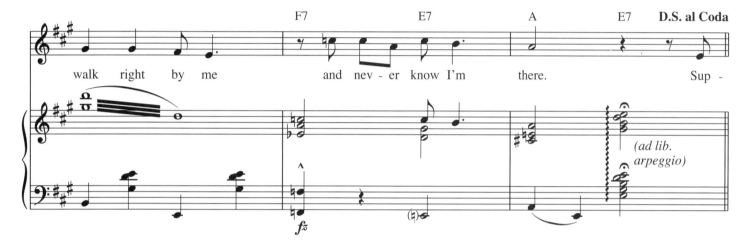

walk right by me and nev-er know I'm there. Sup -

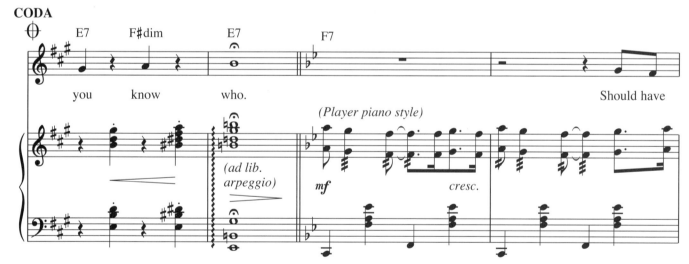

CODA

you know who. Should have

been my name. _ Mis-ter Cel-lo-phane, _ 'cause you can look right thru me, walk with by me,

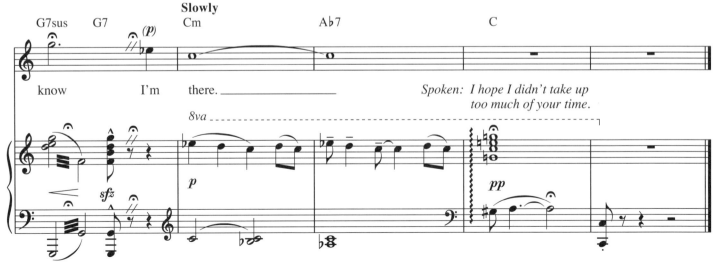

ON THIS NIGHT OF A THOUSAND STARS

from *Evita*

Words by Tim Rice
Music by Andrew Lloyd Webber

In the score of *Evita*, the pianist is directed to "ad lib. (corny night club, Spanish style)."
The right hand in this edition is a simple, written out improvisation.

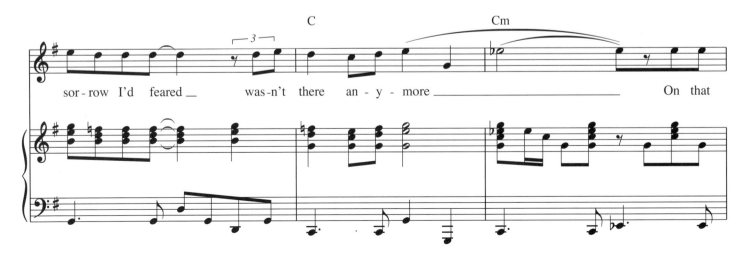

MY UNFORTUNATE ERECTION

from *The 25th Annual Putnam County Spelling Bee*

Words and Music by
William Finn

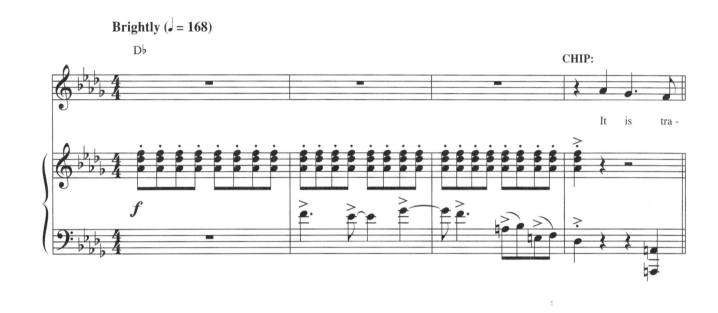

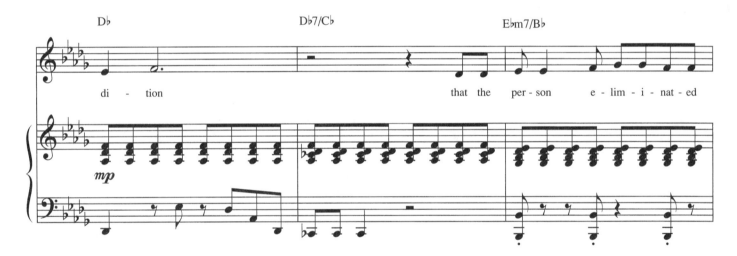

al - pha male, will sell good - ies at the bake sale.

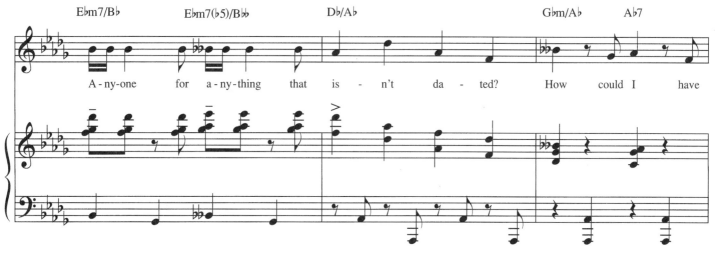

A - ny - one for brown - ies? A - ny - one for choc - 'late chips?

A - ny - one for a - ny - thing that is - n't da - ted? How could I have

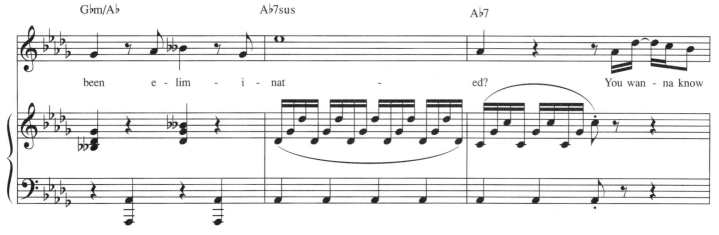

been e - lim - i - nat - ed? You wan - na know

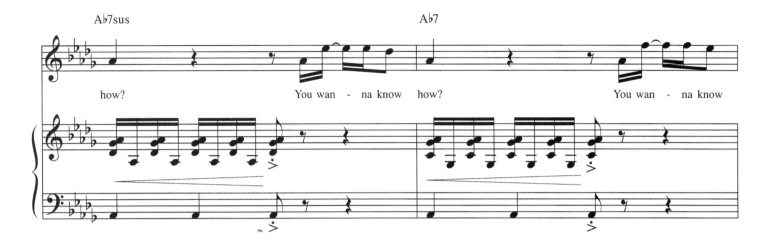

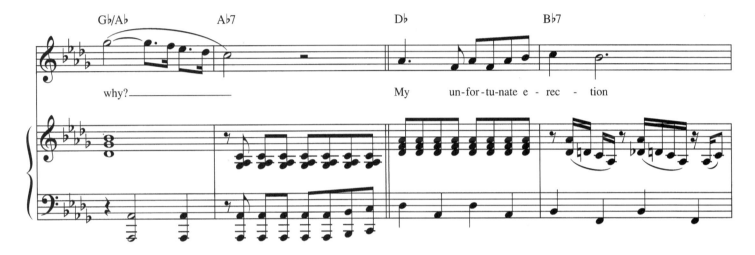

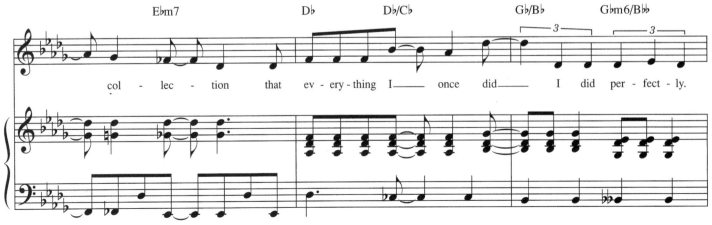

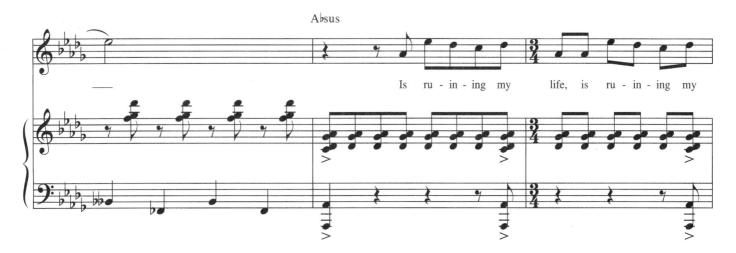

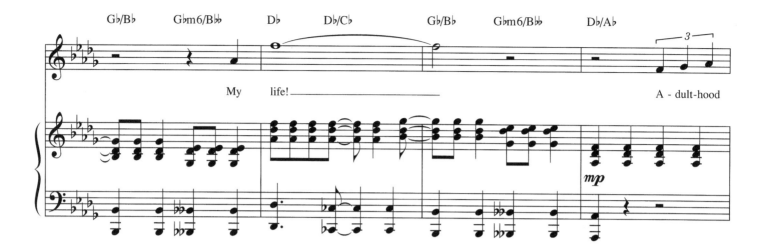

My life!_____

A - dult-hood

brings it's own pe - cu - liar re - jec - tion, which is

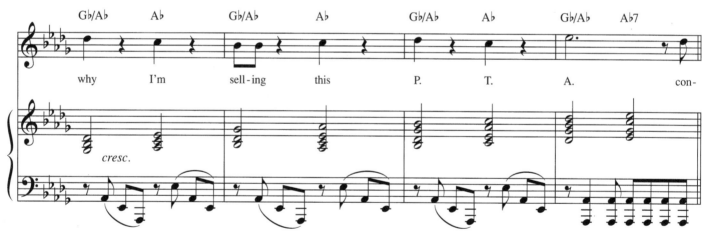

why I'm sell-ing this P. T. A. con-

fec - tion. It will

QUASIMODO

from Howard Crabtree's *When Pigs Fly*

Music by Dick Gallagher
Lyrics by Mark Waldrop

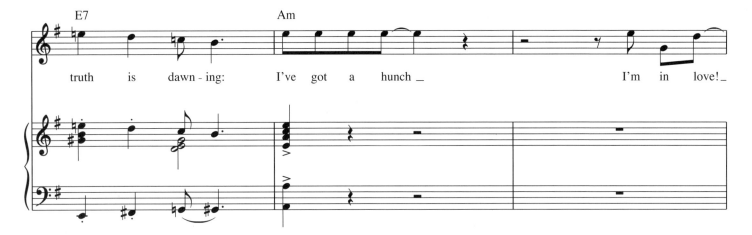

truth is dawn-ing: I've got a hunch ___ I'm in love! ___

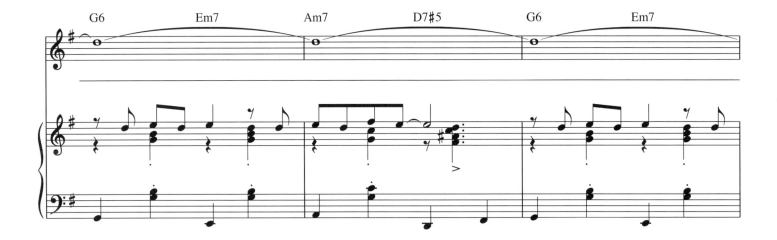

Go tell Mis - ter Vic - tor Hu - go;

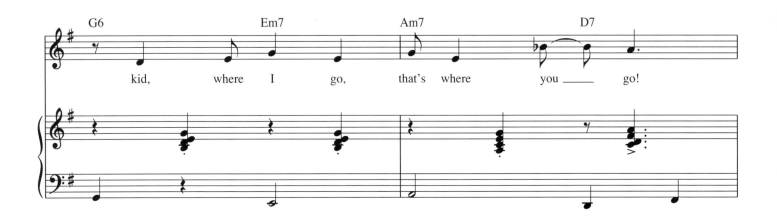

kid, where I go, that's where you ___ go!

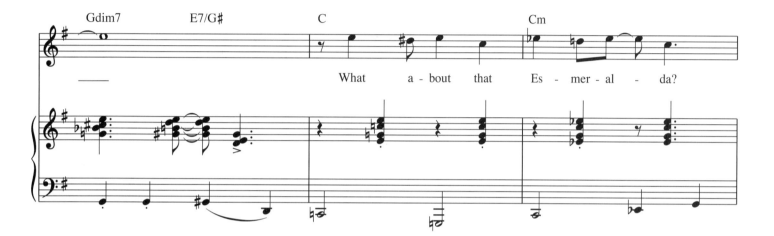

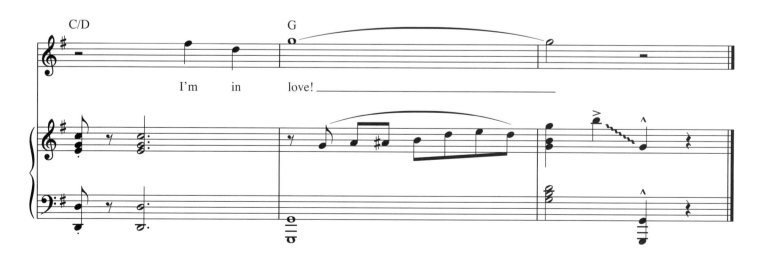

REVIEWING THE SITUATION

from the Columbia Pictures-Romulus Film *Oliver!*

Words and Music by
Lionel Bart

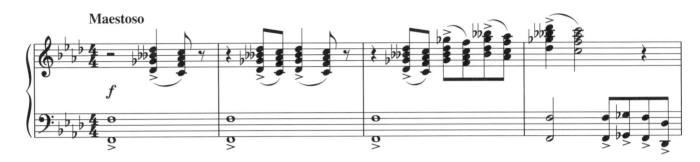

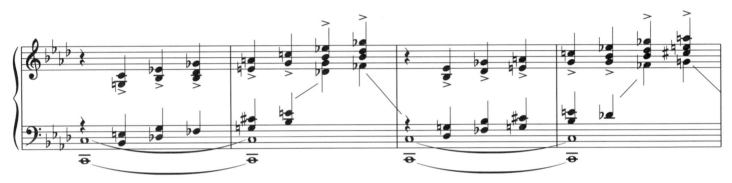

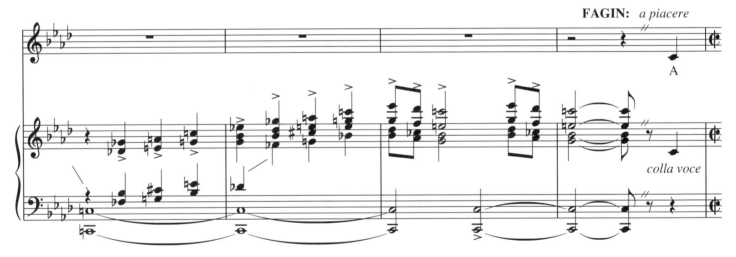

vil - lain all his life?_____ All the tri - als_____

_____ and trib - u - la - tion. _____ Bet - ter set - tle down and

accel. poco a poco

get my - self a wife. _____ And a wife would cook and

accel. poco a poco

sew for me, And come for me and go for me (And *go for me),* and

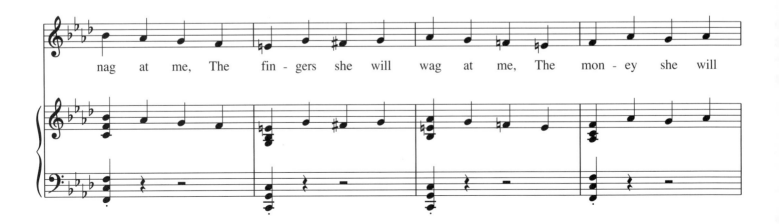

nag at me, The fin - gers she will wag at me, The mon - ey she will

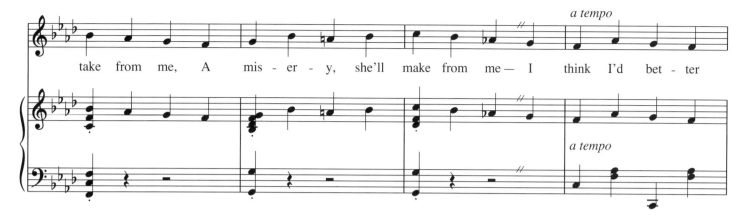

take from me, A mis - er - y, she'll make from me — I think I'd bet - ter

a tempo

think it out a - gain. _____ A

a piacere

colla voce

wife you can keep, an - y-way. I'd rath-er sleep an - y-way, Left with -

out an - y-one in the world and I'm start-ing from now— So

how to win friends and to in-flu-ence peo-ple, so how? ___ I'm re - view-ing ___ the sit - u -

a - tion. ___ I must quick-ly look up ev - 'ry-one I know: ___

___ Ti - tled peo - ple ___ with a sta - tion ___ Who can

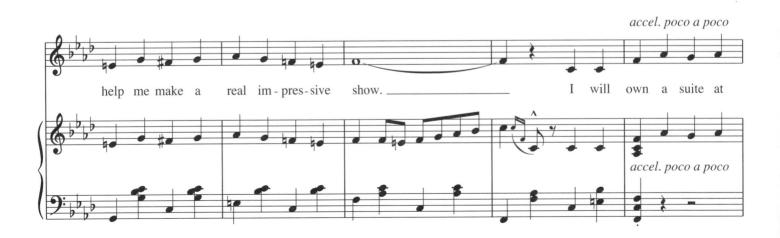

help me make a real im-pres-sive show. ___ I will own a suite at

Cla - ridg - es, And run a fleet of car - riag - es, And wave at all the Duch - ess - es with

meno mosso

friend - li - ness, as much as is be - fit - ting of my new es - tate "Good mor - row to you,

a tempo   *a piacere*

Mag - is - trate!" I think I'd bet - ter think it out a - gain. _____ So

colla voce

where shall I go? Some-bod-y? Who do I know? No-bod-y! All my

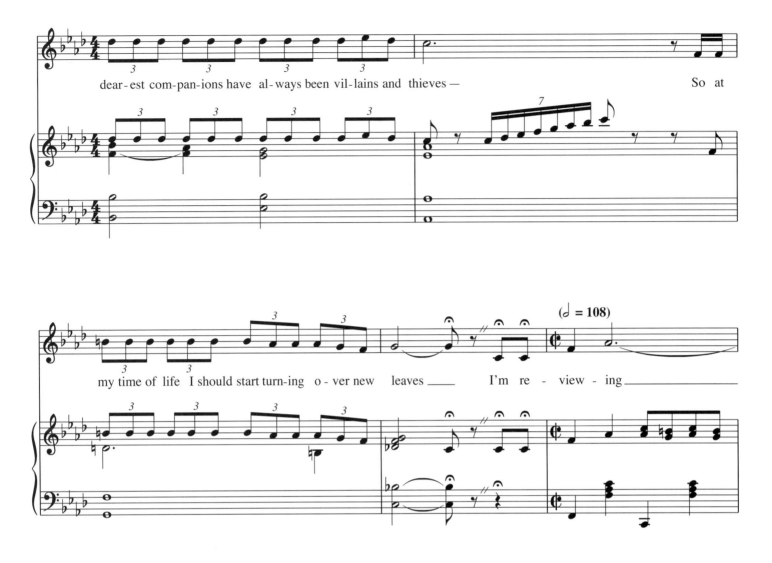

dear-est com-pan-ions have al-ways been vil-lains and thieves — So at

my time of life I should start turn-ing o - ver new leaves ____ I'm re - view - ing ____

($\mathbf{\downarrow}$ = 108)

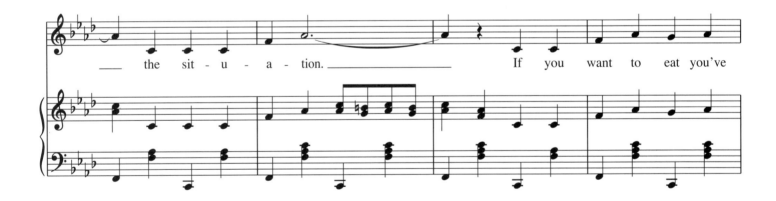

____ the sit - u - a - tion. _____ If you want to eat you've

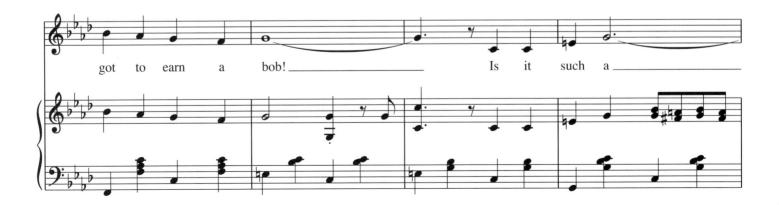

got to earn a bob! _____ Is it such a _____

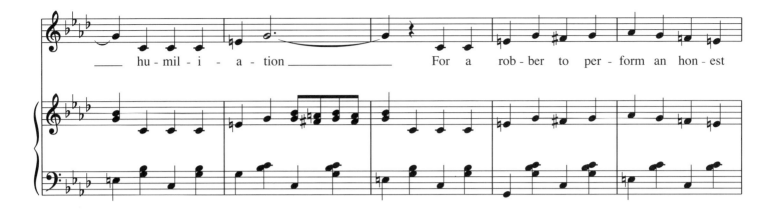

_____ hu - mil - i - a - tion _____ For a rob - ber to per - form an hon - est

accel. poco a poco

job? _____ So a job I'm get - ting pos - si - bly, I won - der how the

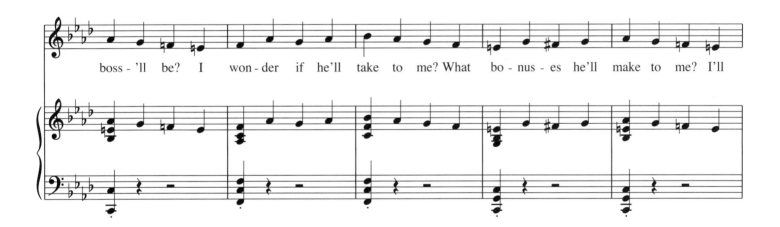

boss - 'll be? I won - der if he'll take to me? What bo - nus - es he'll make to me? I'll

start at eight, and fin - ish late, At nor - mal rate and all, but wait! I think I'd bet - ter

think it out a-gain _____ What hap-pens when I'm

sev-en-ty? Must come a time— Sev-en-ty When you're

old and it's cold and who cares if you live or you die. Your

one con-so-la-tion's the mon-ey you may have put by ___ I'm re-view-ing ___

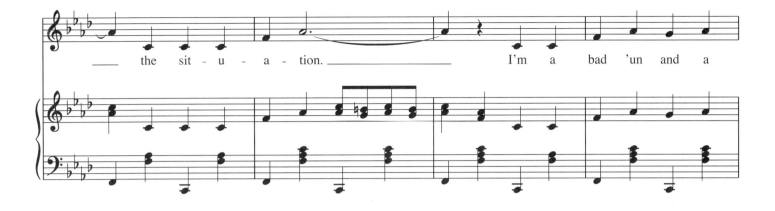

the sit - u - a - tion. _____ I'm a bad 'un and a

bad 'un I shall stay! _____ You'll be see - ing _____

____ no trans - for - ma - tion _____ But it's wrong to be a

accel. poco a poco

rogue in ev - 'ry way. _____ I don't want no - bod - y

accel. poco a poco

hurt for me, Or made to do the dirt for me. This rot - ten life is not for me. It's

meno mosso

get - ting far too hot for me. Don't want no - one to rob for me, But who will find a

rall.

job for me? I don't care what they've got for me. But who will change the plot for ___ me? I

Prestissimo

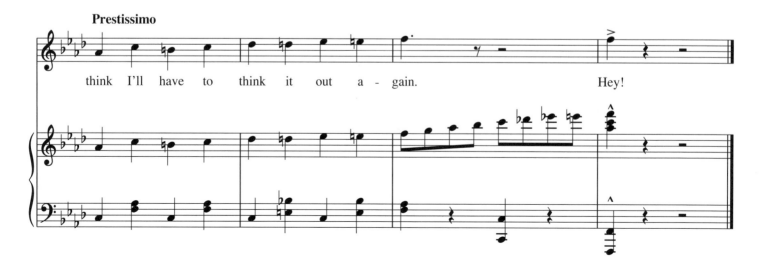

think I'll have to think it out a - gain. Hey!

A SECRETARY IS NOT A TOY

from *How to Succeed in Business Without Really Trying*

By Frank Loesser

Originally for Bratt and ensemble in the show, the song has been adapted as a solo.

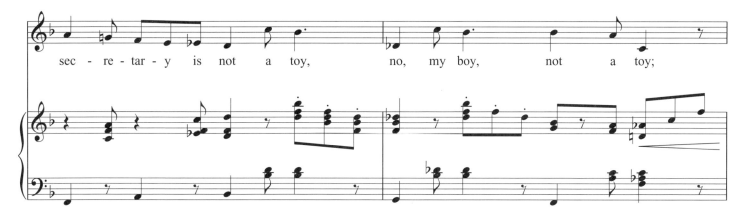

secre-tar-y is not a toy, no, my boy, not a toy;

so do not go jump-ing for joy, boy. A

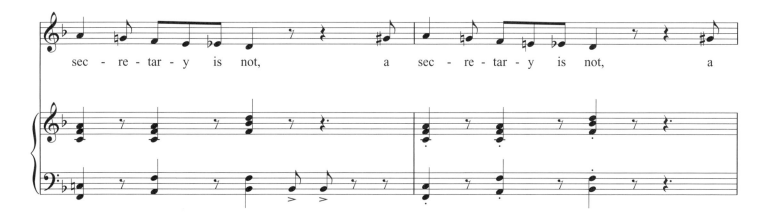

sec-re-tar-y is not, a sec-re-tar-y is not, a

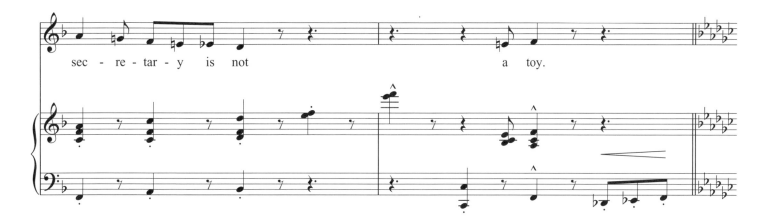

sec-re-tar-y is not a toy.

find noth-ing like her at F. A. O. Schwarz!

A sec - re - tar - y is not a pet,

nor an e - rec - tor set. It

hap-pened to Char - lie Mc - Coy, boy. They fi - red him like a shot... the

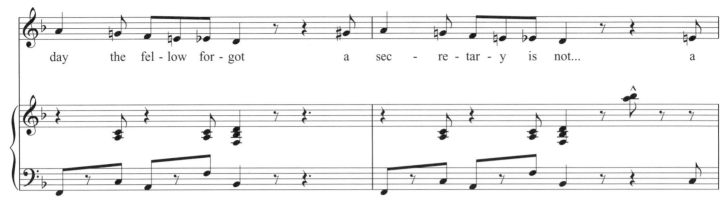

day the fel - low for - got   a   sec - re - tar - y   is   not...   a

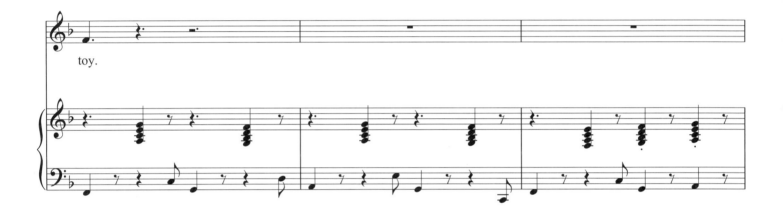

toy.

The   sec - re - tar - y   y' got   is

def - i - nite - ly   not   em - ployed   to   do   a   ga - votte...

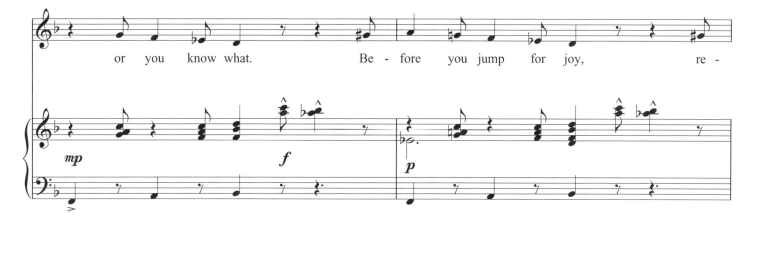

or you know what. Be - fore you jump for joy, re -

mem - ber this, my boy,

(Finger snaps)

rap on piano

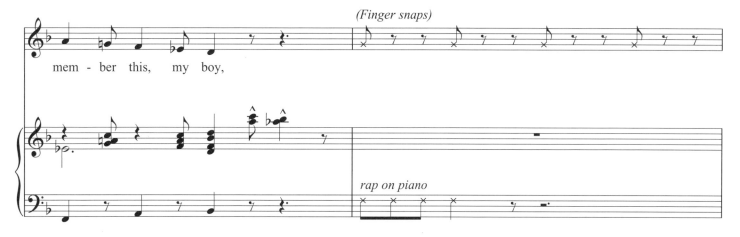

(alternating hands)

a sec - re - tar - y is not...

a tink - er toy!

SIT DOWN YOU'RE ROCKIN' THE BOAT

from *Guys and Dolls*

By Frank Loesser

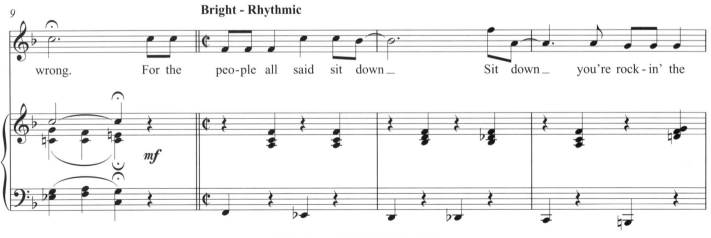

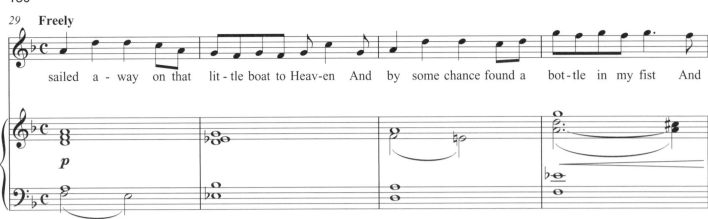

sailed a - way on that lit - tle boat to Heav - en And by some chance found a bot - tle in my fist And

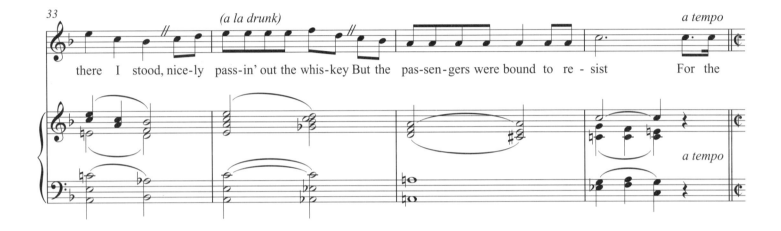

there I stood, nice - ly pass-in' out the whis-key But the pas-sen-gers were bound to re - sist For the

peo-ple all said be - ware, ___ You're on ___ a hea-ven-ly trip,

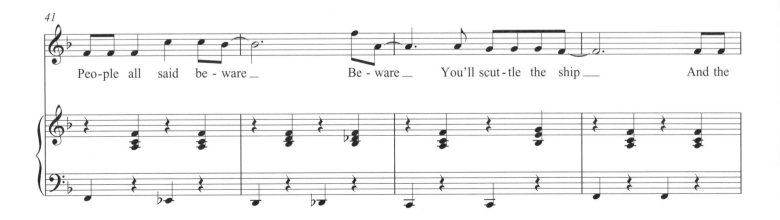

Peo-ple all said be - ware ___ Be - ware ___ You'll scut-tle the ship ___ And the

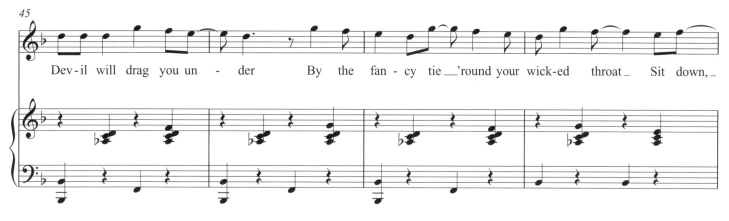

Dev-il will drag you un - der   By the fan - cy tie __ 'round your wick-ed throat __ Sit down, __

__ sit down, __ sit down, __ sit down, __ sit down __ You're rock-in' the boat __   And

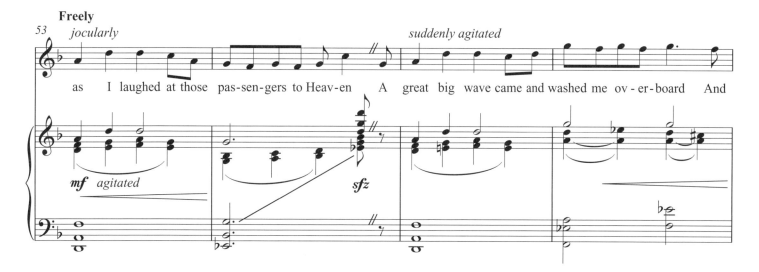

Freely

jocularly   *suddenly agitated*

as   I laughed at those pas-sen-gers to Heav-en   A great big wave came and washed me ov-er-board   And

mf agitated   *sfz*

solemnly   *rit.*

as   I sank And I hol-lered "Some-one save me." That's the   mo-ment I woke up,   thank the

rit.

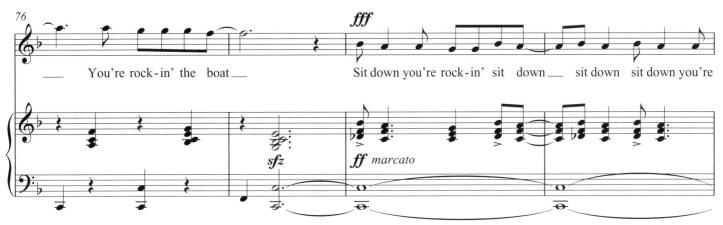

You're rock-in' the boat ___ Sit down you're rock-in' sit down ___ sit down sit down you're

rock-in' the boat ___ sit down you're rock-in' sit down ___ sit down sit down you're rock-in' the boat ___

sit down ___

SPRINGTIME FOR HITLER

from *The Producers*

Music and Lyrics by
Mel Brooks

The Storm Trooper introduces the song in this production number, which has been adapted as a solo.

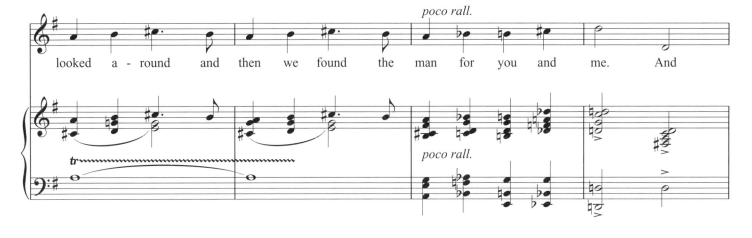

looked a - round and then we found the man for you and me. And

With a lilt, in 4

now it's spring - time for Hit - ler and Ger - ma - ny,

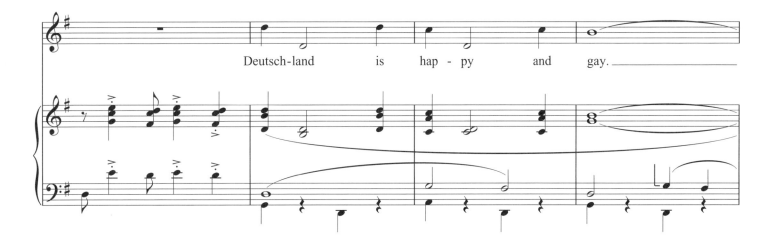

Deutsch - land is hap - py and gay.

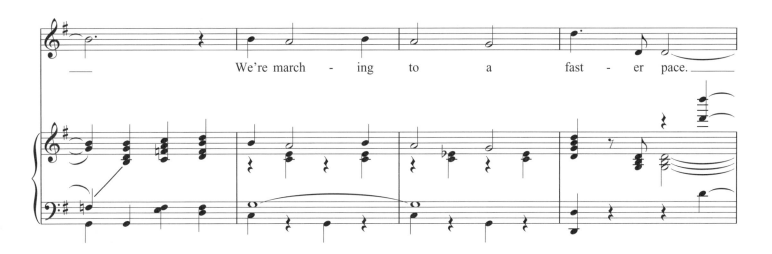

We're march - ing to a fast - er pace.

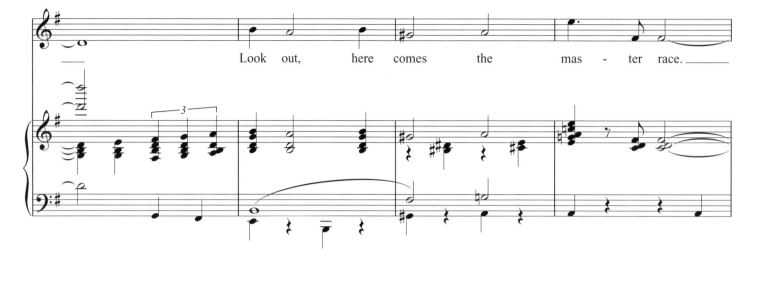

Look out, here comes the mas - ter race. _____

Spring-time for Hit - ler and Ger - ma - ny,

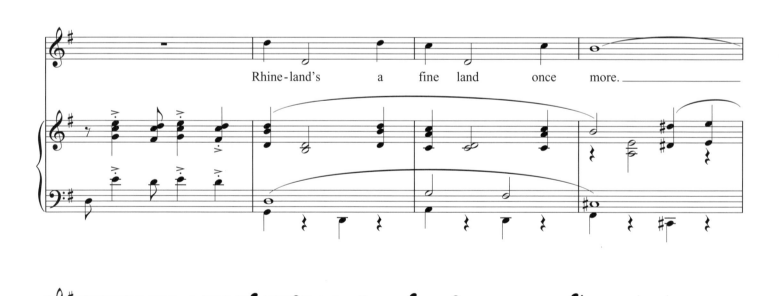

Rhine-land's a fine land once more. _____

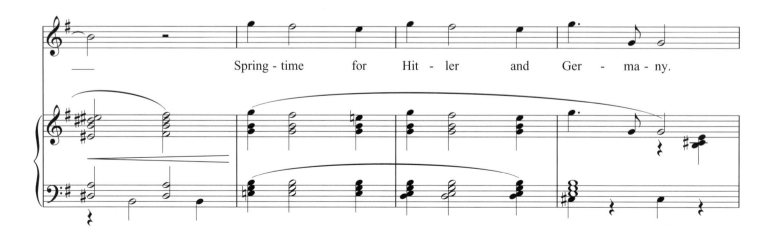

Spring-time for Hit - ler and Ger - ma - ny.

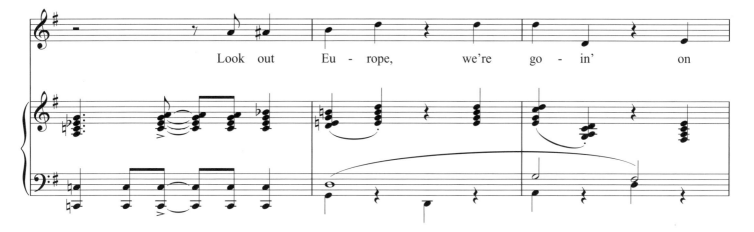

Look out Eu - rope, we're go - in' on

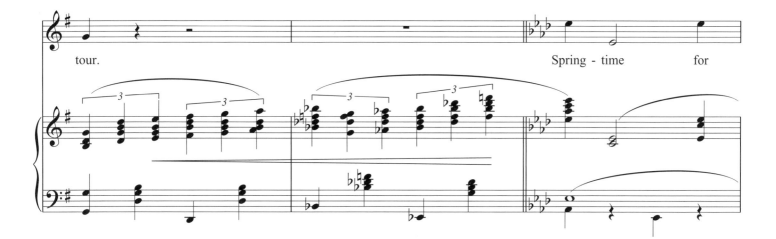

tour. Spring - time for

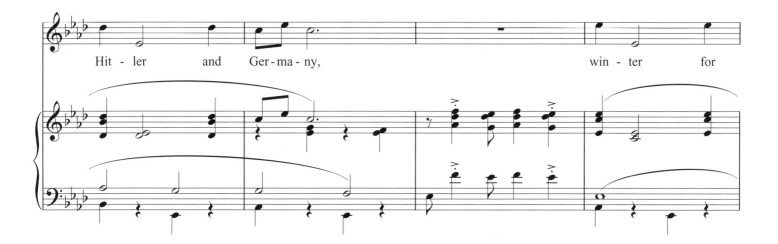

Hit - ler and Ger - ma - ny, win - ter for

Po - land and France. Spring - time for

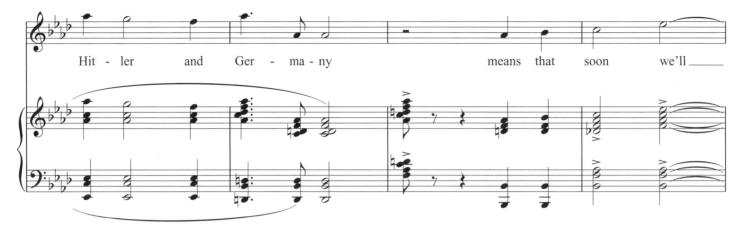

Hit - ler and Ger - ma - ny means that soon we'll

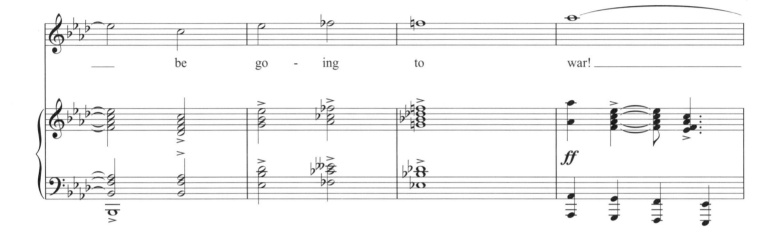

____ be go - ing to war! ____

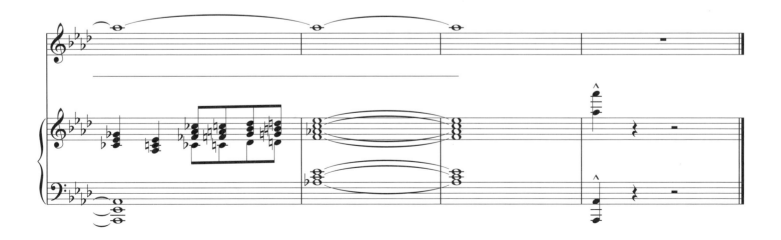

WHERE WAS I WHEN THEY PASSED OUT THE LUCK?

from *Minnie's Boys*

Lyrics by Hal Hackady
Music by Larry Grossman

Funky Gospel Waltz (Swing beat)

This song is sung by the Marx Brothers, adapted as a solo for this edition.

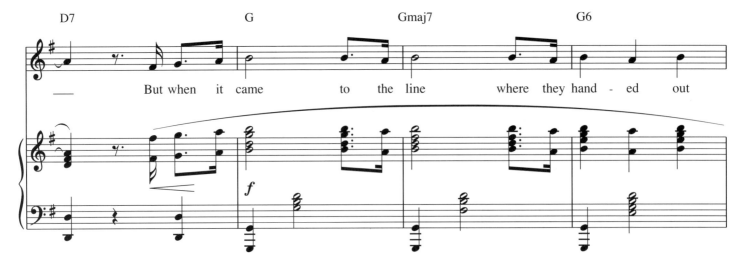

But when it came to the line where they hand-ed out

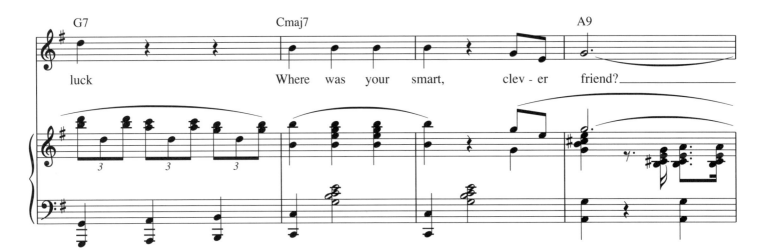

luck Where was your smart, clev-er friend?

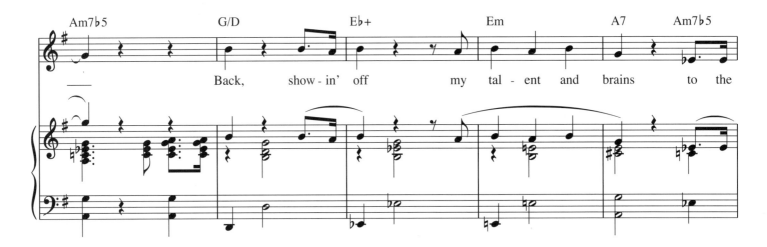

Back, show-in' off my tal-ent and brains to the

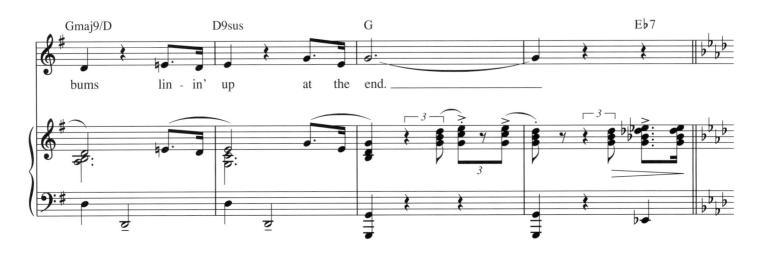

bums lin-in' up at the end.

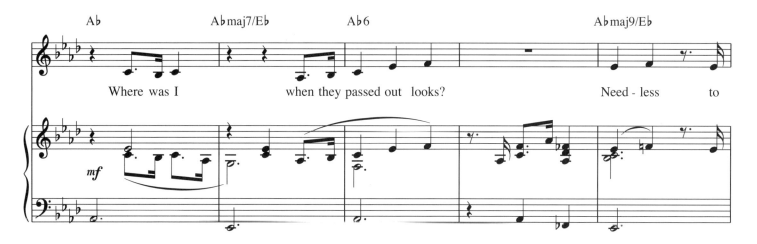

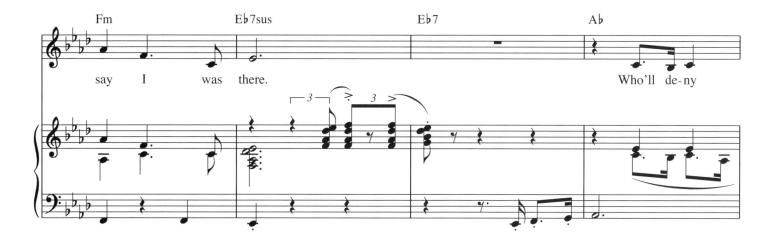

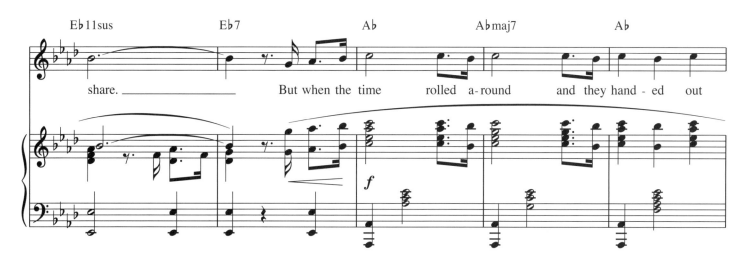

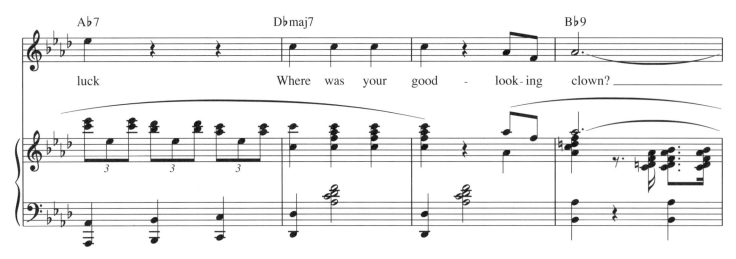

luck   Where was your good - look-ing clown? _____

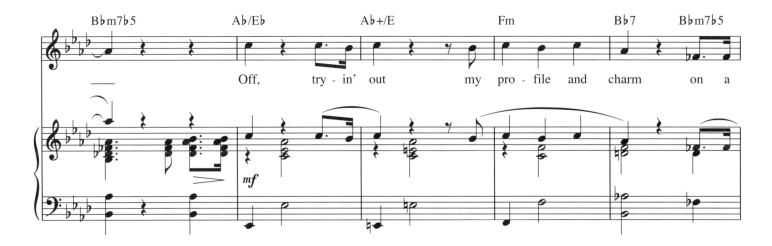

_____ Off,   try-in' out   my pro-file and charm   on a

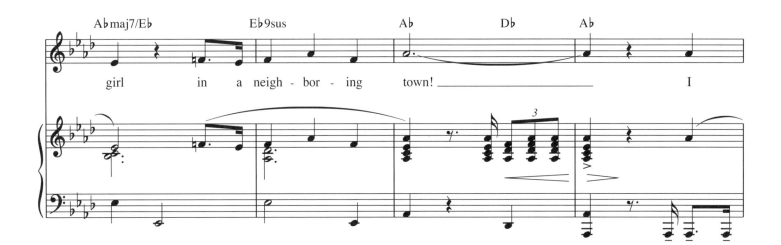

girl   in   a neigh - bor - ing   town! _____ I

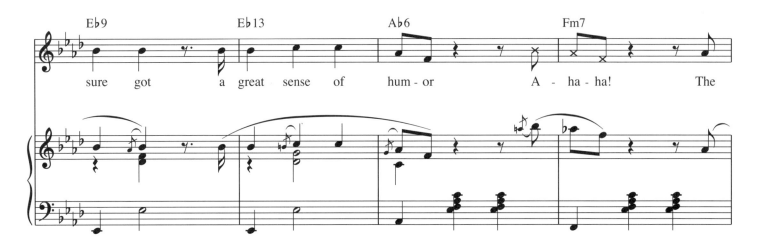

sure got   a great sense of   hum - or   A - ha - ha!   The

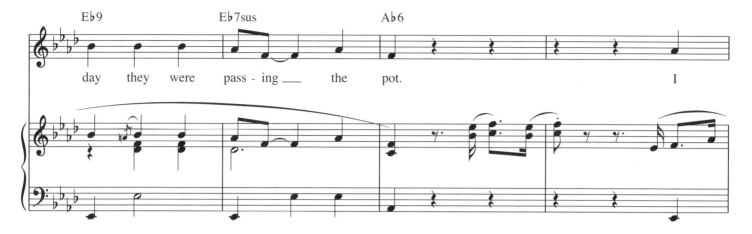

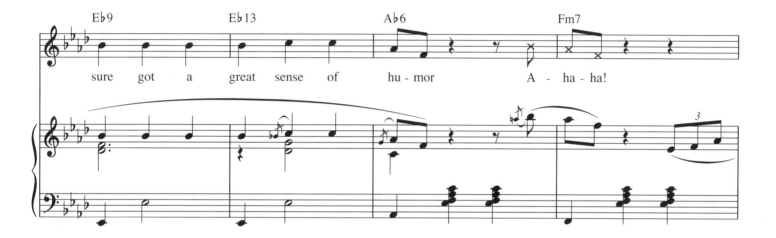

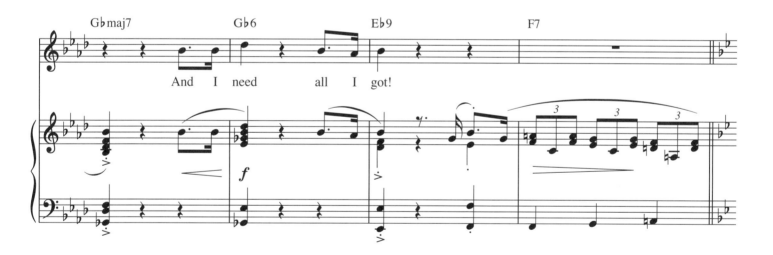

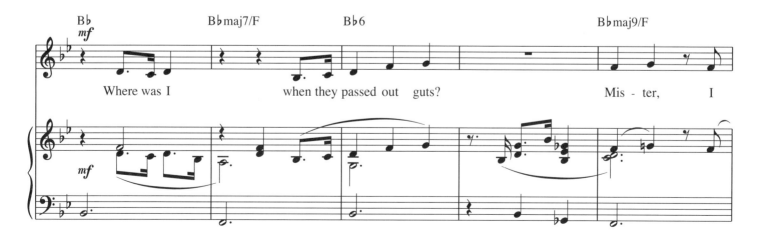

o - pened _ the store! _____ I'm the guy who in-

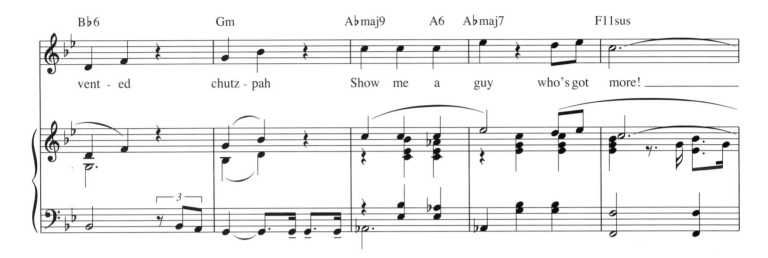

vent - ed chutz - pah Show me a guy who's got more! _____

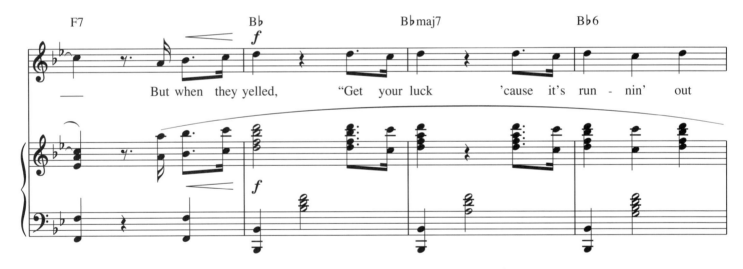

But when they yelled, "Get your luck 'cause it's run - nin' out

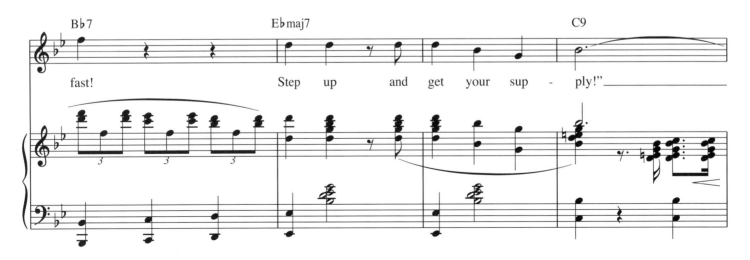

fast! Step up and get your sup - ply!" _____

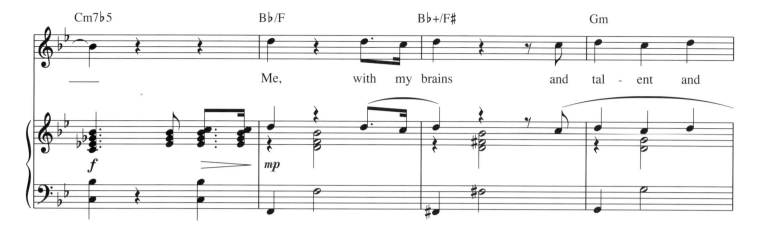

Me, with my brains and tal - ent and

looks Blew the one thing you need to get by! ____

____ Where was I? Where was I? Where was I? Where was

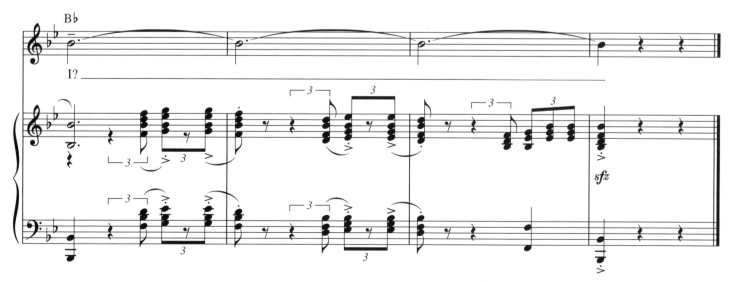

I? ____

YOU WON'T SUCCEED
ON BROADWAY

from *Monty Python's Spamalot*

*Lyrics by Eric Idle
Music by John Du Prez and Eric Idle

Robin is backed up by ensemble, eliminated in this solo edition.

don't have an - y Jews.

You may have dra - ma - tic light-ing, and

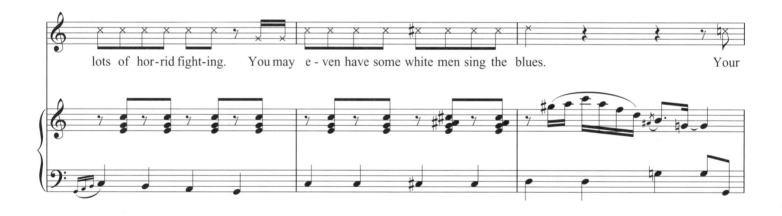

lots of hor-rid fight-ing. You may e - ven have some white men sing the blues. Your

knights may be nice boys, but sad - ly, we're all goys, and that noise that you call sing - ing you must

lose. So, des - pite the pre - ty lights and naught - y girls in nas - ty tights, and the

most im - pres - sive scen - er - y you use, you may have danc - ing *ma - no e ma - no,* you may

bring on a pi - a - no, but they will not give a damn - o if you don't have an - y Jews.

(wailing)

Ah! _____

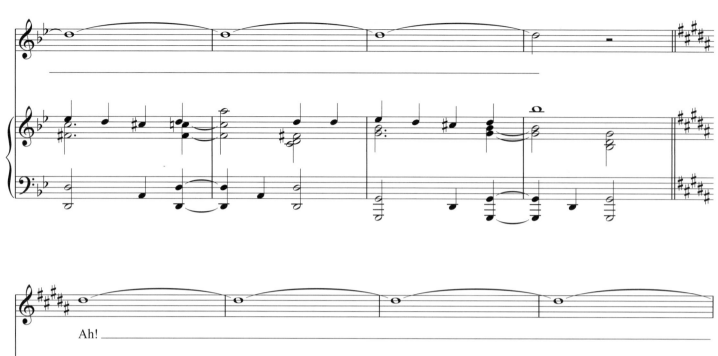

Ah!

You may

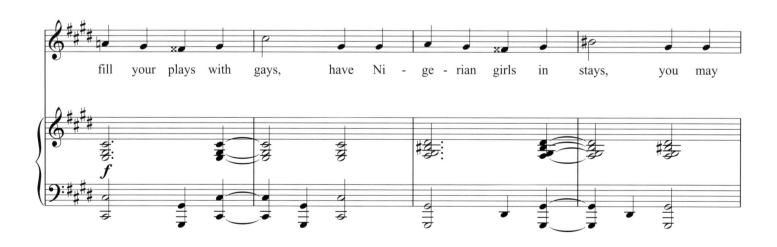

fill your plays with gays, have Ni - ge - rian girls in stays, you may

e - ven have some shik - sas mak - ing stews. You

have - n't got a clue, if you don't have a Jew, all of

your in - vest - ments you are going to lose. There's a

ver - y small per - cen - tile who en - joy a danc - ing gen - tile. I'm

sad to be the one with this bad news.

Nev - er mind your sword - play, you just won't suc - ceed on Broad - way. You just

don't suc - ceed on Broad - way if you don't have an - y Jews.

Kickline tempo

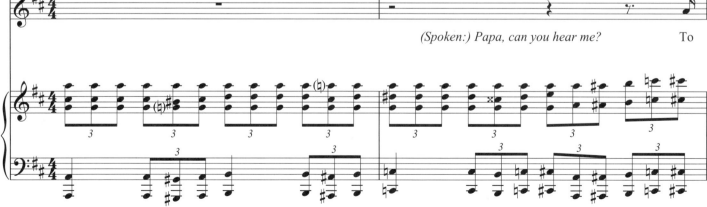

(Spoken:) Papa, can you hear me? To

get a-long on Broad-way, to sing your song on Broad-way, to hit the top on Broad-way and not

lose. I tell you, Ar-thur King, there is one es-sen-tial thing: There

sim-ply must be, sim-ply must be Jews.

There sim-ply must be, Ar-thur, trust me, sim-ply must be Jews.